BARBRA·THE FIRST DECADE

BARBRA · THE
THE FILMS AND CAREER

FIRST DECADE
OF BARBRA STREISAND

By James Spada

CITADEL PRESS BOOK

Published by Carol Publishing Group

A Citadel Press Book
Published by Carol Publishing Group

Editorial Offices
600 Madison Avenue
New York, NY 10022

Sales & Distribution Offices
120 Enterprise Avenue
Secaucus, NJ 07094

In Canada: Musson Book Company
A division of General Publishing Co. Limited
Don Mills, Ontario

Manufactured in the United States of America
ISBN 0-8065-0515-X

15 14 13 12 11 10 9 8

ACKNOWLEDGEMENTS

A special debt of gratitude is owed Mr. Christopher
Nickens of Hollywood, California, whose extensive
collection of Barbra Streisand memorabilia contrib-
uted many of the stills used in this book. Others
whose help is greatly appreciated are: The staff of
the Lincoln Center Library of the Performing Arts,
Roberta Twombly, Robert Chiarello, Vito Russo, Lou
Valentino, Peter Black, Francine and Stephen Doody,
Larry Paulette, Jim Parish, Bill Kenly, Abba Bogin,
Miles Kreuger, Craig Zadan, Don Koll,
Ken Moses, Lynn Dorsey, Richard D. Kennedy, Mike
Ruvo, Gregory Downer, Bill Guastavino, Ralph
Quevereaux, Karen Weissmuller. The movie stills in this
book are courtesy of the producing studios. Photos from
Another Evening with Harry Stoones by Avery
Willard. Location photos from Up The Sandbox, The
Way We Were and For Pete's Sake by Robert
Chiarello. Photos of Barbra in London are copyright
by the Daily Express, Daily Mirror and Associated
Newspapers, Ltd. London stage photos copyright
Dominic Photography, Ltd. New York stage photos
courtesy of Friedman-Abeles and Gene Andrewski.
Television stills courtesy CBS-TV. Mad satire copyright
© 1971 by E.C. Publications, Inc. courtesy Mad Maga-
zine. Other photo sources were Cinemabilia, United
Press International, Movie Star News, The University of
Texas at Austin, Las Vegas Hilton and Columbia
Records. Album covers reproduced through the
courtesy of Columbia Records.

TABLE OF CONTENTS

FOR BARBRA

Sing thou smoothly with thy beauty's
Silent music, either other
Sweetly gracing.

Thomas Campion

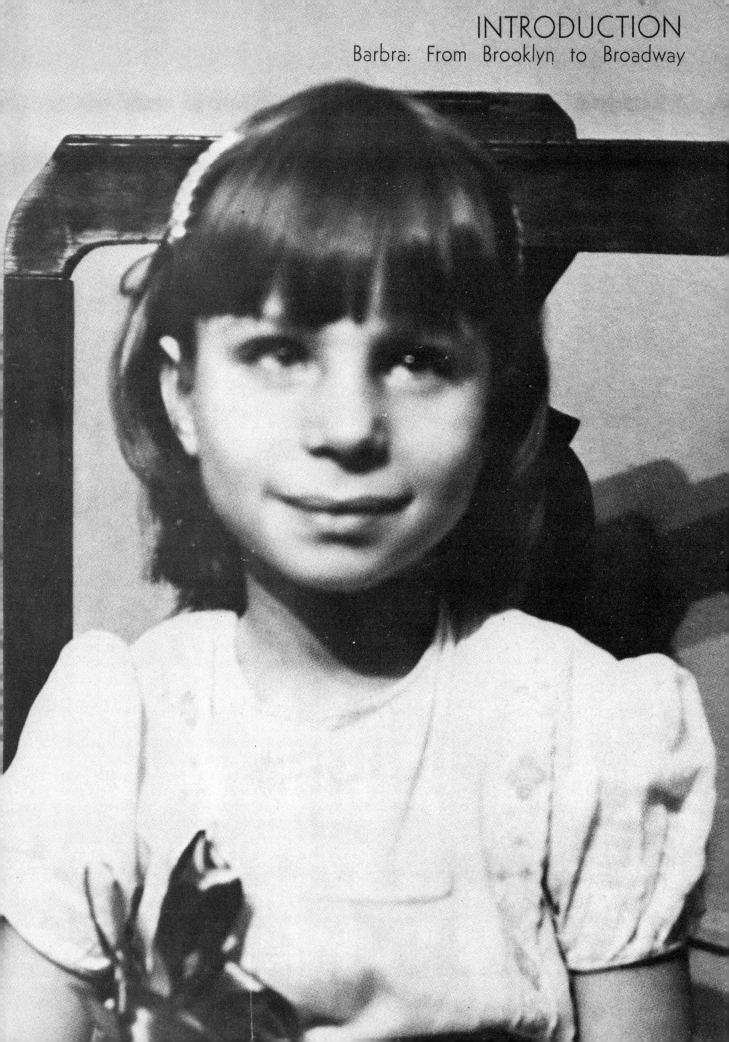

Barbara at age 5, wearing an Indian outfit made by her brother Sheldon.

Barbra Streisand's first decade in show business has been one of unparalleled success. In ten short years, and before her thirtieth birthday, she had conquered Broadway, London, the recording industry, the concert circuit, television and finally and most triumphantly Hollywood. A superstar in a generation otherwise without them, she is a star in the great tradition of stars, inspiring fierce loyalty and worship not seen since the days of Marilyn Monroe and Judy Garland.

Under any circumstances, Barbra's magnificent talents—a beautiful, pure singing voice and marvelous comedic timing—would have made her a star. That she has transcended that designation can be traced to many diverse elements of her personality, and the public's.

Streisand's story is the epitome of the American Dream. She is the homely, awkward, lonely outsider with pent-up talent who has to fight rebuffs, skepticism and outright rejections in order just to be heard, and whose determination and faith in herself keep her going until she makes it to the pinnacle of success. This Cinderella tale, told by Barbra with a flair after her initial Broadway successes, struck a responsive chord in the American public, and it helped to make her an object of cult-worship by millions. She was the embodiment of their dreams, their one hope that they too might succeed against the odds, and they became her loyal partisans.

But unlike Cinderella, Barbra Streisand stayed a Princess. Or rather, she evolved into one. By the time she made her first film, *Funny Girl*, the homely and awkward young girl was being called beautiful and graceful, and she *was*. It wasn't the beauty which left-handed compliments had called "the beauty of her talent," it was true beauty, and while certainly not in the classic Hollywood mold, it was nonetheless real.

Like so many of the great stars before her, Barbra Streisand has *screen presence*: that indescribable magic which makes it virtually impossible to watch anyone else when she is on screen. Her personality comes across beautifully on celluloid. She is alternately vulnerable, coy, charming, sexy, glamorous and endearing. She can thus at the same time make women want to emulate her and men want to protect her. Most of all, she makes people want to *see* her: in an era of which it has been said, "There are no stars anymore; today, the plot's the star," Barbra Streisand is, in the words of Pauline Kael, "a complete reason for going to a movie."

Barbra Streisand has captured the imagination of the American public as few before her have done. To better understand how she was able to do this, we must return to Brooklyn, New York, where she was born on April 24, 1942.

Diana and Emanuel Streisand named their second child Barbara Joan. She was a healthy baby and nicely rounded out the Streisand family group, brother Sheldon having been born eight years before. The Streisands were a happy, close and moderately successful family. Mr. Streisand was a professor of English and Psychology with a Ph.D. in Education from Columbia University; Mrs. Streisand was a devoted wife and mother. The family's outlook was indeed promising, but within fifteen months of baby Barbara's birth, the idyl was shattered: Emanuel Streisand suffered a cerebral hemorrhage and died.

Mrs. Streisand took her husband's death very hard. She supported her children on her brother's army allotment checks until they stopped, then she went out to work as a bookkeeper. Now, the family's existence was meager. There was enough money for the basics, but little left over for anything else. As Barbra said later, "We were poor, but not *poor* poor. We just never had anything."

More than any other event in her life, the death of her father set the stage for the person Barbara Joan Streisand was to become. Attempting once to explain it, she said, "When a kid grows up missing one parent, there's a big gap that has to be filled. It's like someone being blind, they hear better. With me, I felt more, I sensed more, I wanted more. . . ."

As she grew older, this sensitivity left Barbara unusually vulnerable to the cruelties of other children. She was, in many ways, different, and to most children *different* is *bad*. Young Barbara's painful shyness, her large nose and skinny frame, her awkwardness and somewhat crossed eyes made her the butt of constant taunting and unkind remarks. She was called "big beak" and "crazy Barbara." Few children would befriend her, preferring to jump on the bandwagon of ridicule, and Barbara knew loneliness at a very early age.

To escape the tauntings, Barbara spent most of her time in the family's apartment in a six-story building on the corner of Newkirk Avenue and Nostrand Avenue, where they had moved shortly after Mr. Streisand's death. But with her mother working and her brother too busy with his own friends to give his young sister the attention she required, there was little her own home could offer her. Her desire for more from life made her situation seem even worse than it was, and as she grew older and more independent, she began to hate the plainness and loneliness of her home.

Her one respite from this life and environment would come on Saturdays, when she would run down to the Loew's Kings Theatre, the neighborhood movie house. There, she sat before the great screen and saw life as it should be: beautiful, perfect—just the opposite of her life. For two hours she would leave the reality she knew and escape into the fantasy world before her. She would become the characters on the screen, and she was happy—but only for a short time. Once the film ended, reality abruptly returned, and her existence seemed only worse through comparison. "It was terribly depressing," she says.

By the time she reached her early teens, Barbara began escaping her drab existence more often than just at the Saturday movies. She created her own fantasies at home, usually re-creating the roles she had just seen played out on the screen. "I was a character in the movie," she says. "Not the actress, but the character. Not Vivien Leigh but Scarlett O'Hara. I loved being the most beautiful woman kissed by the beautiful man."

Although Barbara's fantasies began as a supplement to her routine and lonely days, they soon started to take over her personality, to become more than just a game. Standing in front of her bathroom mirror, she imitated commercials she had seen on television. She experimented with

Age 12, at her graduation from P.S. 89 in Brooklyn.

The corner of Newkirk Avenue and Nostrand Avenue, where the Streisand family moved after Mr. Streisand's death.

STREISAND, BARBARA
Freshman Chorus. 1, 2: Choral
Club. 2-4.

cosmetics, using assorted shades of lipstick and eyeshadow to create different characters and fashionable "looks" for herself. She went to neighborhood thrift shops and bought thirty-year-old dresses, feather boas and floppy hats, using money she had saved by forgoing school lunches. On the roof of her building, she sang popular songs and read lines from plays, taking on several of the roles.

Such "play-acting" soon evolved into a firm decision: She was going to be an actress. She would escape from Brooklyn and her life there; she would become loved instead of taunted; she would be famous and glamorous. Such visions weren't, as they are for most would-be actors and actresses across America, nebulous wish-dreams. For Barbara, they were a *goal*, and one she began working toward early. Now, her experiments with make-up, her period costumes, her line readings were no longer just escapes from loneliness, they were her *preparation*: "I used to spend a lot of time and money in the penny arcades taking pictures of myself in those little booths. I'd experiment with different colored mascara on my eyes, try out all kinds of different hairstyles and sexy poses." Barbara began wearing her strange thriftshop outfits to school, each day with a new make-up and hair-do. "Somehow," she says, "it made me think I was attractive."

Rather, Barbara's unusual appearance and behavior served only to further alienate her from her classmates at Erasmus Hall High School and drive her deeper and deeper into her private world. In what was by now a vicious circle, the laughter and jeers directed at her only made Barbara strive to be even more different—as if to "give them something to laugh about." Although she graduated from Erasmus with a 93 average and a medal in Spanish, school never really appealed to her. She rarely took part in any school activities, not even, despite her theatrical aspirations, the drama club: "Why go out for an amateurish high school production," she remembers thinking, "when you can do the real thing?"

The "real thing" came in 1957 when, after her sophomore year, she traveled up to Malden, New York, and applied for a summer stock position with the Malden Bridge Playhouse. She was accepted, and between

Erasmus Hall High School, from which Barbara graduated in 1959.

The Loew's Kings Theatre on Flatbush Avenue, where young Barbara Joan Streisand dreamed of being on screen.

assignments as janitor and stagehand appeared in *Picnic*, rode horseback in *Teahouse of the August Moon* and played a coquettish young girl in *The Desk Set*: "Can't you just see me at fifteen, coming on stage, sitting down on a desk, swinging my legs and playing sexy?" Barbara's fantasies were beginning to come true.

But the summer had to end, and Barbara returned to reality, to the apartment where she slept on the living room couch and didn't have a Victrola to practice her singing with. Matters weren't improved by her mother's remarriage to Louis Kind, a used car salesman. Barbara virtually ignored him, and she rarely speaks of him today. When she does, it is negatively: "He disliked me." She spent little of her time at home; after school she worked in Choy's Chinese Restaurant—"I loved the idea of belonging to a small minority group. It was the world against us in the Chinese restaurant." On Saturdays, she worked as an usherette—"I hid my face when I directed people to their seats, because I knew I'd be famous one day, and I didn't want the embarrassment of having any of them think later: 'Oh yeah, *her*, the star. She used to be an usherette at the neighborhood theatre. . . .' "

Barbara's apparently arrogant self-confidence was, of course, a defense, a shield against the doubts and ridicule which surrounded her. None of her friends or classmates believed she would be successful, and her mother attempted to discourage her ambition, fearing she would be hurt. "I didn't think she was pretty enough," Mrs. Kind says. "There was no security." She would point out her daughter's shortcomings in an effort to dissuade her, but this only had the reverse effect on Barbara: "The more she said I'd never make it, that I was too skinny, the more determined I got." When her mother suggested she'd be happier as a secretary, she grew her fingernails several inches long, "so I *couldn't* learn to type!"

Barbara soon decided that she would have to make a clean break with Brooklyn and her life there if she were ever to make her dreams come true. After graduating from high school in January 1959, she announced her intention to move to Manhattan and seek work in the theatre. Her mother was at first vehemently opposed—"I thought it would be a fiasco" —but finally relented when she realized how determined her daughter was. "I let her get an apartment with a friend," Mrs. Kind remembers. "I would call her all the time, much to her annoyance, and find out where she was living so I could bring her chicken soup."

Finding out where Barbara was living wasn't always that easy. When the apartment sharing didn't work out, she started carrying a cot around with her and sacking out wherever she could—in friends' apartments, public relations offices, studio lofts. Her attempts to find work in the theater resulted in a floor sweeping job at the Cherry Lane Theatre. There she met Mrs. Alan Miller, whose husband was a noted drama coach.

Mrs. Miller saw possibilities in Barbara, and introduced her to her husband. He agreed to coach Barbara if she would babysit with the Millers' son Greg. At one of their dramatic sessions, Miller told her to portray a chocolate chip melting in an oven. "The whole point," Barbra says, "was to experience something organically, to lift it from an intellectual level and give it a physical life." Miller recalls that Barbara's portrayal was ". . . beautiful, so tender. We saw Barbara not awkward and unsure, but as she felt in her imagination."

The Millers, however, had little inkling of another talent of Barbara's. "We never knew Barbara could sing until we were invited to hear her . . . but Greg once or twice remarked, 'Barbara's been singing again.' "

At the same time, Barbara was studying with another coach, Eli Rill, whom she told her name was Angelina Scarangella so he wouldn't realize she was studying with anyone else. Rill found her aspirations misdirected. Rather than trying to develop what he saw as her innate comic talents, Barbara would become angry if the class laughed when she performed. "I kept telling her," Rill says, "that she had to develop what she had and not try to be somebody else. She would make it clear that my role was to make her a tragic muse."

Both Rill and Miller soon told Barbara that she would have to start "making the rounds" of theatrical auditions if she were ever to find work as an actress. She immediately did so, and was singularly unsuccessful. With her strange looks, personality, and clothes, few people would give her a hearing. "I was usually abruptly dismissed," she says. "People looked at me as though I was nuts. I'd say, 'Look, you'd better sign me up, I'm terrific.' But they wouldn't let me read. How could they tell anything if they wouldn't let you read? I couldn't even get hired as a beatnik."

Most of the people she went to see told her to change herself—fix her nose, discard the outlandish outfits, subdue her Brooklyn accent. Barbara would have none of it. They would have to take her as she was or not at all. Her "kookiness," she says, was "a big, defensive, rebellious thing. But at the same time, it was *theatrically right* for me. I *knew* it." The only thing she would consent to change was her name, and even then, rather than totally discarding it, she simply removed an "a" from Barbara, thereby making Barbra Streisand just a little more unique. She took delight in her new appellation. Later, she would tell reporters "I don't care what you say about me. Just make sure you spell my name wrong." Keeping her real name was important to her, "because I wanted all the people I knew when I was younger to know it was me when I became a star."

Truly discouraged by all the rejections she had encountered at auditions, Barbra renounced the theatre, saying, "They'll have to come to me." Although she hadn't given much thought to singing, she knew she had a good voice and thought perhaps she could at least make some money at it. In the spring of 1961, primarily due to economic necessity, she entered a talent contest at the Lion, a bar and restaurant on Ninth Street in Manhattan. First prize was $50.00 and a week's singing engagement. Meals were included. "That's all I had to hear," says Barbra, "and I decided to enter the contest. I've made many a deal based on a meal." She chose the ballad "A Sleepin' Bee." After practicing it, she tried her rendition out on several friends. "I was so embarrassed, I couldn't sing in front of them, so I asked if they wouldn't mind, I'd sing facing the wall. When I finished, and turned around, I remember I couldn't understand why they had tears in their eyes."

At the contest, Barbra easily defeated another pop singer, a light-opera singer and a comedian. The pop singer has since remarked, "With her there, the rest of us didn't have a chance."

Barbra's performances at the Lion caused a sensation. Her unique appearance—she had by now dyed her hair red and wore chalk white make-up—amazed and delighted her audiences. Out she would come, fresh from a thrift-shop shopping spree, in somebody's cast-off evening gown, wearing ancient dangling jewelry, black fish-net stockings and long red fingernails. Barbra's material was as unique as her appearance—a bouncy version of "Who's Afraid of the Big, Bad Wolf?" complete with whoops and tra-la-las; the absurd ditty "Come to the Supermarket in Old Peking"; a delightfully mischievous "Keepin' Out of Mischief Now."

Her voice was pure and lovely, big enough to put across the most theatrical number and soft and mellow enough to tug at the heartstrings

Barbra singing at the Bon Soir, (photographed by Craig Simpson).

Performing at Basin Street East, 1961

with the most romantic ballad. Her range was phenomenal. Before long, people were coming to the Lion just to see *her*. But once her short engagement was over, she was immediately signed by the Bon Soir, a better-known Greenwich Village nightclub, where her initial salary was more than doubled, to $125.00 per week.

She was an even bigger sensation at the Bon Soir, introducing new material and outfits nightly. The first night she performed, she was wearing a $4 black dress, a $2 Persian vest and old white satin shoes with large silver buckles. On her second night, her mother came to see her. "I wore a white lace combing jacket from 1890 with pink satin shoes from the twenties," Barbra says. "My mother was sure I was singing in my nightgown. But to me it was beautiful."

Off-Broadway producer Burke McHugh was present at one of Barbra's early Bon Soir appearances, and remembers her unique entrance: "She asked to be introduced as Barbra Streisand from Smyrna, Turkey, and when she took the floor she let out a piercing shriek. That got attention. She paused, took a wad of gum from her mouth, deftly stuck it to the microphone for safe-keeping, and launched into 'Who's Afraid of the Big, Bad Wolf?'"

To get new and different songs, Barbra would call music publishers and say she was Vaughn Monroe's secretary: could they send over some complimentary sheet music? The gambit worked.

During her engagement at the Bon Soir, Barbra met Marty Erlichman, a struggling talent agent. Erlichman, a large, friendly man, immediately sensed a tremendous future in this singular young girl and offered to represent her. What resulted was one of Barbra's most important professional associations and one of the most mutually profitable partnerships in show business history.

Barbra's initial two-week engagement at the Bon Soir stretched to eleven as more and more people flocked to see this singer who was quickly becoming the talk of the New York nightclub circuit. She not only had a beautiful voice, fresh material and a fascinatingly strange appearance, but she infused all her songs with an intense, personal quality. Because her main desire was to be an actress, Barbra treated each song as a role to be performed, interpreted: "I thought, I'm an actress and what am I doing here singing? Until I realized each song is another play, another character. When I used to sing 'Cry Me a River,' I had a specific person in mind. I tried to re-create in my mind the details of his face."

Because of her own involvement in her songs, Barbra involved all the members of her audiences in them as well. One talent scout, sent to hear her, reported back to his boss that "Streisand sang five songs, and I got goose bumps on three of them. It was amazing."

The patrons at the Bon Soir soon learned that Barbra's uniqueness wasn't entirely an act. Whenever anyone would offer to buy her a drink she'd reply, "I'd rather you bought me a baked potato."

Barbra was pleased with her success as a singer. "I got a special sort of satisfaction out of singing," she says, "because all of a sudden ... well, in life I felt that people didn't pay any attention to me. ... On stage, singing, I could say what I felt, and I was listened to." And her differences, for which she had been cruelly taunted as a child, were being not only accepted, but acclaimed. She wasn't, however, completely happy. She still wanted to be on the stage—"I'm not a singer. I'm an actress who sings." After eleven wildly successful weeks at the Bon Soir, she went to one more audition for an off-Broadway revue. This time, she wasn't abruptly dismissed—she got the part.

Another Evening with Harry Stoones was a farcical, free-wheeling off-Broadway revue for which Barbra's unique talents were ideally suited. Its songs, sketches and blackouts were topical, irreverent and, in some cases, off-color. The show's creator, Jeff Harris, was a Harvard graduate whose last assignment had been playing a homicidal maniac on the daytime TV soap opera *The Edge of Night*. Because of the type of show *Stoones* was, Harris found it "impossible to cast": "We searched for actors who could sing, actors who could move, and above all, actors who could make us laugh. It was only after many weeks of suffering and muffing that we found the rare, wildly talented actors we had been looking for."

After Barbra's audition, which had been arranged for her by Marty Erlichman, Jeff Harris turned to the show's musical director, Abba Bogin, and said, "Let's grab her. She's fantastic." Among others in the show's cast who went on to renown were Diana Sands, who was later to originate the role of Doris in *The Owl and the Pussycat* on Broadway, and Dom De Luise, who has become a highly successful television comedian.

The revue's title had no meaning, and when asked why he chose it, Harris replied, "It fit the mood of the show better than, say, *A Streetcar Named Desire*."

Barbra was featured in nine sketches and sang three solos and a duet with Dom De Luise. Her roles included a 1920s flapper, an Indian squaw and Peter Pan's Wendy. In one song, "Jersey," she sang of her need to get to her boyfriend by traipsing through New Jersey's most preposterous sounding cities—Hackensack, Hohokus, etc.—and she imparted a terrible desperation to the number, frantically running around the stage. One sketch called "Party of the First Part" concerned a birthday party for young Wendell Mootz, and another, "Minnesota," was a parody of "Oklahoma" in which every name in America beginning with "Minnie" was used—all the way from Minnetonka to Minnie Mouse. One of Barbra's solos, "Value," in which she weighs the advantages of one rich boyfriend against the other, stopped the show on opening night, Saturday, October 21, 1961. Unfortunately, that proved to be the closing night as well. The Mondy morning papers carried pans of the show from *The New York Times* and the *Herald Tribune*, and the producers, short of cash, were forced to close it. As it turned out, later that week *Women's Wear Daily* and *The New Yorker* carried excellent reviews, and the show might have survived if it had been able to get through that first week.

With Kenny Adams

16

The cast of Another Evening with Harry Stoones. *Left to right, Sheila Copelan, Virgil Curry, Susan Belink, Diana Sands, Barbra, Ben Keller, Kenny Adams and Dom De Luise.*

Abba Bogin feels the show was hurt too by the out-of-the-way location of the Gramercy Arts Theatre. "But most of all," he adds, "the show failed because it was too far ahead of its time. It had none of the Noël Coward traditionalism revues always had to have, and people just weren't ready for a lot of the off-color humor. Today it would be a smash. It was just too avant-garde."

Several of the critics reviewing *Another Evening with Harry Stoones* singled Barbra Streisand out for praise, but almost all spelled her name with the extra "a."

Once *Stoones* closed, Barbra put her disappointment behind her and immediately accepted an offer to sing at the Blue Angel, a mid-town showcase frequented by show business personalities and producers. She continued to wow audiences in her inimitable style, and many of her audiences were soon largely comprised of talent scouts, producers and directors who were looking for new faces and had heard of this remarkable young girl.

One of these was Arthur Laurents, who was set to direct a new Broadway musical for David Merrick, *I Can Get It For You Wholesale*. One of the characters in the Harold Rome musical, based on Jerome Weidman's best-selling novel of the garment industry, was Miss Marmelstein, a secretary described in a casting announcement as "nearsighted, harried and efficient." Laurents thought this strange young girl with the big voice would make a perfect Yetta Tessye Marmelstein, and he immediately arranged for an audition.

With Sheila Copelan

After performing one number and reading some lines at her audition, Barbra began handing out her telephone number to the other actors assembled in the theater. She explained that she had just had her first telephone installed that morning, and wanted someone to call her.

That night, alone in her thrift shop paraphernalia-littered apartment, Barbra got her first phone call. A male voice said: "You asked for someone to call you, so I called. I just want to tell you, you were brilliant today."

The caller was Elliot Gould, the former chorus boy of *Irma La Douce* who had been tapped to play the lead in *Wholesale*. Gould had seen Barbra for the first time at her audition and later said, "I thought she was the weirdo of all times." But, "the more I got to know her, the more I was fascinated with her. She needs to be protected. She's a very fragile little girl. . . . I found her absolutely exquisite. . . ."

Their courtship began immediately. The couple took long walks throughout New York City, attended innumerable midnight horror movies, spent many nights searching for diners with Barbra's favorite, rice pudding without raisins. Soon Elliot moved into Barbra's apartment after learning to cope with the aroma arising from the fish store directly below. Within a year of their first meeting, they were wed.

In the meantime, Barbra was chosen to play Miss Marmelstein. Harold Rome was so impressed with her at the audition that he added a song to the score just

I Can Get It For You Wholesale—With Elliot Gould, Marilyn Cooper and Lillian Roth

for her, "Miss Marmelstein," which lamented the secretary's anonymous existence.

Just before *Wholesale* opened, Barbra was asked to fill out a questionnaire for the biographical capsule which was to appear in *Playbill*, the theater program magazine distributed to all Broadway patrons. She returned the form to press agent David Powers, indicating that she was "born in Madagascar and reared in Rangoon." Powers remembers, "I was annoyed. There were ten biographies to write, hers was the last in the program, I thought I had a wisecracker, so I let it go. I thought she'd be annoyed. She was absolutely delighted. The only trouble was, she wanted to insert a different birthplace in *Playbill* every week. *Playbill* was annoyed. They like facts."

There was, however, a method to Barbra's madness. As she explained it, "The audience would read it before I came on and notice me more. I played the part of a Brooklyn girl and if I had said Brooklyn, well . . ." As it was, the biography listed Zanzibar and Aruba before finally admitting, three months after the show opened, that she was "born and reared in Brooklyn, New York."

By the time Barbra had performed the "Miss Marmelstein" number on opening night, March 22, 1962, the audience was certain it was witnessing the debut of an exciting new musical comedienne. For this, her one solo number, Barbra entered in a swivel chair, her back to the audience, a pencil stuck in her bee-hived hair. She was wearing an incredibly dumpy dress and when she turned around, her expression was the epitome of dour dissatisfaction. "Oh *why* is it always *Miss Marmelstein*?" she asked plaintively, and in each performance she won the hearts of another audience.

Although *I Can Get It For You Wholesale* received mixed reviews, Barbra's performance was unanimously hailed. The view of one critic that Streisand "sets this show in motion and hypos it all the way" was shared by audiences, and Barbra's performance and the attendant excitement surrounding her "discovery" were credited with keeping the show open for as long as it ran, nine months.

And excitement there was. Practically overnight, Barbra began appearing in national magazines, attending important parties and making guest appearances on television, first on local New York shows, then nationally on the "Tonight Show." She won her first award, the New York Drama Critics' prize as "Best Supporting Actress in a Musical," and was nominated for a Tony Award.

The Streisand voice was soon immortalized in wax. Her "Miss Marmelstein" was the highlight of the Original Cast recording of *Wholesale*. At almost the same time, she performed on the 25th Anniversary album of another Harold Rome musical, *Pins and Needles*, which was also about the garment industry. By fateful coincidence, both of these were produced by Columbia Records.

During the *Wholesale* run, New York newspapers carried a story that Barbra was planning to attend Dartmouth College in the fall of 1963, when that school would begin accepting women for the first time. "It's not that I don't like Broadway," the stories quoted Barbra, "it's just that I want to develop myself into a human being. Only then can I really be an actress."

Once *Wholesale* closed on December 9, 1962, however, Barbra must have dropped any such plans

while being besieged with offers from nightclubs, TV
and Broadway producers. After marrying Elliot Gould
in March, she embarked on a nightclub tour which
took her from New York to Chicago to San Francisco.
Her salary, once $50.00 a week, was now $7,000 a
night. She made appearances on the television shows of
Bob Hope, Judy Garland, Dinah Shore and Ed Sullivan. Her growing legion of fans included President
John F. Kennedy, who invited her to sing at the
White House Press Correspondents' Dinner in May.
Introduced to the President, Barbra looked at him and
said, "You're a doll."

Streisand's hectic pace continued into the summer,
when she played a series of smash engagements on the
West Coast. She enraptured audiences at the Coconut
Grove, Harrah's at Lake Tahoe, the Hollywood Bowl
and the Riviera at Las Vegas. Although her fashions
now were more traditional, the singularity of her voice
and material continued to entrance audiences. Her
reception at the Riviera typifies this. Opening the
dinner show (an unenviable assignment), Barbra,
rather than singing the traditional up-tempo number
designed to lure the audience's attention away from
their dinners, began with "When the Sun Comes Out,"
a haunting ballad. Composer Sammy Cahn described
the reaction: "I was just getting over the shock of it
when I noticed, to my amazement, that everyone had
stopped eating. Even more amazing, the waiters had
stopped serving. It was all Barbra Streisand, and Barbra
Streisand had them all."

At "the hungry i" San Francisco.

She was taking the country by storm. Audiences
were coming in droves to see and hear her, reporters
and photographers were following her everywhere,
fans crowded her for autographs. Under a new contract to Columbia Records, she had released two sensational albums which topped record-sales charts for
months.

*...ing a gingham dress she de-
...for her Coconut Grove act.*

The culmination of her tour was her first one-
woman concert at Chicago's 5,000-seat Arie Crown
Theatre, a sold-out triumph. During one of her
numbers, the Streisand humor emerged as she stopped,
looked out at the vast throng and said, "I wish I had
the popcorn concession in this place."

After Barbra returned to New York late in 1963,
it was announced that she had copped the plum of the
1964 Broadway season, the role of Fanny Brice in
Funny Girl. With all this, it came as little surprise
when Barbra was named *Cue* magazine's "Entertainer
of the Year." The magazine aptly summed up the
general reaction to Barbra's first two years in show
business: "In nightclubs and on television, on Columbia
Records and in the theatre, *La* Streisand is a champ."

Funny Girl originated as a biography culled from
notes the great *Ziegfeld Follies* star Fanny Brice had
dictated shortly before her death in 1951. Her son-

(Photos by Craig Simpson)

...r. Kelly's" in Chicago during her 1963 nightclub tour.

in-law, movie producer Ray Stark, paid $50,000 to
have the book plates destroyed in order to turn the
Brice story into a screenplay. Finally, it became a play
by Isobel Lennart, which Stark planned to produce as
his first Broadway venture.

Anne Bancroft, who had shortly before won a
Best Actress Oscar for *The Miracle Worker*, was
slated to play Fanny. At rehearsals, however, Miss
Bancroft discovered that her voice could not project
the powerful numbers as required, and she bowed out.
By this time, Barbra Streisand had come to the atten-
tion of Stark. Many people who remembered Fanny
Brice were remarking that Barbra strongly evoked
memories of her earthy, Jewish comedy. Stark
instantly agreed, and Barbra was signed to play Fanny.
Sydney Chaplin, Charlie's son, was to play Nick
Arnstein, Fanny's gambler husband.

The production encountered difficulties from the
very outset of rehearsals. The character of Nicky
Arnstein created a problem: how to make a basically
seedy, small-time gambler with a cavalier attitude
toward his wife's love and devotion a suitably sympathetic leading man? The answer was a dashing figure
who turns to crime only to save his masculine self-
esteem when he finds himself becoming too dependent
upon his wife. Unfortunately, what was gained in
audience sympathy was lost in character substance.
Through dozens of rewrites, Nicky Arnstein became
more and more a cardboard figure, and *Funny Girl*
became more and more a one-woman show.

The one woman, Barbra Streisand, was burdened
with demands few fledglings to Broadway stardom
could have supported. Songs were added, scenes
rewritten, interpretations changed day to day. The
show opened in Boston and was widely criticized.
More rewrites, more new songs, $30,000 worth of new
sets. Director Garson Kanin's efforts were supple-
mented by director Jerome Robbins, hastily brought in
as "Production Supervisor."

The early troubles weren't all with the music,
libretto, sets and direction. Some of them were with
the star. At the beginning of the fifteen-week out-
of-town tryouts, Streisand ran through her songs and
scenes perfunctorily, showing little flair for stage
comedy. But as the show plodded toward Broadway,
she picked up inflections, gestures and rhythms which
began to make her performance a comic delight.
Through Barbra's inspiration, the seduction scene,
originally played straight, became the marvelously
funny farce it is.

Streisand's interpretation of Fanny Brice was
characteristically unique. She didn't try to imitate the
Ziegfeld star: "I've never seen her or heard her," she
said. "When the show closes, that's when I'll listen to

all her old records and see any movies she was in. But in the show, I approach the character as though she was not an actual person. . . ." The result, as one critic later pointed out, was "a 1918 Barbra Streisand."

After five postponements, *Funny Girl* opened at the Winter Garden Theatre on March 26, 1964. All the delays, revisions and troubles proved more than worth it. The evening was one of the most memorable and exciting in theater history. Barbra was nothing short of magnificent, and the critics were nothing short of rapturous in their praise: "Everyone knew Barbra Streisand would be a star," wrote Walter Kerr, "and so she is." *Cue* magazine began its review, "Magnificent, sublime, radiant, extraordinary, electric —what puny little adjectives to describe Barbra Streisand."

New York quickly fell in love with Barbra. In rapid succession she appeared on the covers of *Time*, *Life*, *Show* and *Cosmopolitan*. Before long, the "Barbra Streisand Look"—pageboy hairstyle, Cleopatra eye makeup, billowy dresses—was sweeping the country, and she appeared in the pages of *Vogue* as a fashion model three times in 1964 alone. The Encyclopaedia Britannica chose Barbra as one of the two fashion trend-setters of 1964. Could Barbra still be considered "kooky?" Fashion editor Eugenia Sheppard wrote: "She's only about as kooky as Gloria Guiness, C-Z Guest, the Duchess of Windsor or any of the all-time fashion greats when they had just turned twenty-two."

With Lee Allen in a scene from Funny Girl.

Backstage on opening night of Funny Girl *with Fanny Brice's brother Lew (left) and her children Frances (Mrs. Ray Stark) and Bill.*

Barbra visits Carol Channing backstage at Hello, Dolly!

Craig Simpson's 1961 photo of Barbra seems to preview her Funny Girl *look of 1964.*

Barbra's career was going in higher and higher year. She was nominated for a Tony Award as Best Actress in a Musical. She sang for President Johnson at his inaugural. She won several Grammy Awards for her first album, and four more Streisand records were in release and selling at Gold Record paces. She was signed to a multi-million dollar contract by the Columbia Broadcasting System, calling for her to star in one television special per year for ten years.

And all the time she continued to wow SRO audiences at the Winter Garden. Crowds milled around the stage door after each performance, hoping to catch a glimpse of her. Celebrities visited her backstage almost daily: Audrey Hepburn and Mel Ferrer, Elizabeth Taylor and Richard Burton, Lauren Bacall and Jason Robards, Julie Andrews, Marcello Mastroianni. Frank Sinatra paid her a visit and then sent her a fan letter: "You were magnificent. I love you."

Barbra's stardom in *Funny Girl* soon transcended mere popularity. She became an object of intense followings—people who trailed her everywhere, read everything they could about her, emulated her. This "cult worship" was somewhat predictable in light of Barbra's early struggles for fame. The story of the homely, awkward girl with the magnificent voice who had to fight so hard to be heard made great newspaper copy. It was a Cinderella tale, and Barbra told it with a flair. The Streisand story struck a responsive chord in the public, and as her reputation grew, so did her following. She was a symbol to millions of star-struck young would-be actors and actresses who saw in Barbra's success their great hope. After Streisand, they could realistically feel it wasn't necessary to be beautiful to succeed, to follow all the rules in order to break into show business. Barbra Streisand thus filled a need in these people, and they became, and remained, her loyal partisans.

Barbra left *Funny Girl* after nearly two years on December 25, 1965, in order to re-create the role in London. After her triumph on Broadway, on records, and in her first television special, she was by now the most publicized performer in America, and was being called the highest paid entertainer in the world. She entered the United Kingdom amid a whirlpool of ecstatic press accounts of her successes and popularity. The London critics were in a "show me" mood when *Funny Girl*, the most publicized show in the history of London theater, opened at the Prince of Wales Theatre on April 13, 1966.

Show them Streisand did. British critics threw their restraint to the winds in praising Barbra's performance. One said, "Barbra Streisand performed the daunting feat of living up to her legend. The girl and the myth are indivisible." Another asked the inter-

With her poodle Sadie, a gift from the cast of Funny Girl.

esting question "Who will they get to play her when the time comes for a musical on her life?" The London Drama Critics voted Barbra the Best Foreign Actress and *Funny Girl* the Best Foreign Musical of 1966.

Funny Girl was attended by almost every celebrity then in Europe. Most made it a point to visit Barbra backstage and offer their congratulations.

During one such visit, Sophia Loren told Barbra, "I would give anything if I could sing like you." To which Barbra replied, "If I could *look* like you, I wouldn't even wanna talk!" When Barbra was introduced to Queen Elizabeth II, the Queen said, "I have all your records." All Barbra could manage in response to that was, "Yeah?"

Barbra cuts the cake at a farewell party th... for her by Funny Girl's London cast.

Arriving in London with Elliot for Funny... run.

...rforming at Georgia's Atlanta Stadium during her last public appearance tour before retiring to await the birth of her ...t child.

Barbra dotes on newborn Jason, December, 1966.

Two months after the opening, Barbra and Elliot announced the impending birth of their first child. It was front-page news on two continents. The child was immediately dubbed "Barbra's Million Dollar Baby," because her pregnancy would force her to cancel a million dollars in concert tours scheduled for later that year. On December 29, 1966, a son, Jason Emanuel, was born to the Goulds. Barbra calls London "the city that gave me Jason, love and a little piece of forever."

Barbra's *Funny Girl* run in London was contracted to be fourteen weeks, and every performance was sold out. Her pregnancy forced her to miss several shows, much to the dismay of audiences. After one such announcement, 400 people stalked out of the theater and demanded their money back. Such was Streisand's drawing power that immediately after she left the show, it closed. Before she left London, the cast threw a farewell party in Barbra's honor. To make her feel at home, they had hot dogs, sauerkraut, pastrami and potato knishes flown in from Nathan's of Coney Island.

The London production of *Funny Girl* proved to be the last time Barbra appeared on a legitimate stage in a performing capacity. Will she ever do another Broadway show? In London, she told her co-star Michael Craig, "Two and a half years ago when I started this show in Philadelphia, it was such fun and everything was marvelous. Now it's all so difficult and I don't get any fun out of it anymore." She has also said that she finds it difficult facing live audiences and performing every night. So it is unlikely that Barbra will ever do another play, although there is no dearth of offers for her return. Should the perfect vehicle arrive, Barbra just might change her mind.

"Big Barry"

"Jersey," one of Barbra's solos.

With Sheila Copelan, Diana Sands and Susan Belink

CAST

Diana Sands
Sheila Copelan
Dom De Luise
Ben Keller
Kenny Adams
Virgil Curry
Susan Belink
Barbra Streisand

CREDITS

Music and Lyrics by   Jeff Harris
Musical direction and accompaniments by   Abba Bogin
Choreography by   Joe Milan
Settings and lighting by   Robert E. Darling
Costumes by   Ruth Wagner
Entire production staged by   G. Adam Jordan
Presented by   Stenod Productions, Inc.

Opened October 21, 1961, at the Gramercy Arts Theatre

PROGRAM OF SONGS AND SKETCHES

PART ONE—THE CIVIL WAR

Carnival in Capri	*Entire Cast*
To Belong	*Kenny*
Communication	
Waiter	*Dom*
Lulu	*Diana*
Jose	*Ben*
Cook	*Kenny*
Ballad to the International	
Business Machine Building	*Virgil*
You Won't Believe Me	*Sheila*
The Wrong Plan	*Diana*
Ballet	
Wendy	*Barbra*
Michael	*Kenny*
Nana	*Dom*
Peter Pan	*Harriet All*
Bang!	*Susan*
Don't Laugh at Me	*Virgil & Diana*
Museum Piece	*Dom*
Tableau	
Christopher Columbus	*Virgil*
Sailor	*Ben*
Indians	*Sheila, Susan & Barbra*
Indian Nuts	*Diana, Sheila, Susan & Barbra*
Uh-Oh	*Kenny, Virgil & Dom*
Ragtime	*Abba*
Minnesota	*Entire Cast*
Ballad of the Tree	*Virgil*
Value	*Barbra*
Session	
Bonnie	*Diana*
Hillary	*Sheila*
Allie	*Kenny*
Isidore	*Ben*
Man	*Virgil*
My Doggie	*Dom*
Jersey	*Barbra*
Dancin' Free & Easy	*Diana & Kenny*
Dr. Rosalyn Green	*Sheila*
Invitation to the Basketball	*Ben*
Party of the First Part	
Wendell Mootz	*Kenny*
Alfie	*Dom*
Nancy	*Barbra*
Arthur	*Ben*
Barbara	*Susan*

PART TWO—THE ROARING TWENTIES

Big Barry	
Ace	*Ben*
Jimbo	*Dom*
Barry	*Kenny*
Tina	*Sheila*
Jo-Jo	*Diana*
Nancy	*Barbra*
Miss Greenwich Village	*Susan*
Stephanie	*Dom*
Betty Simpson	*Sheila*
The Rage	*Susan, Virgil, Barbra & Kenny*
Upstairs at the Downstairs	*Diana*
Hail to Thee!	*Kenny, Barbra, Susan & Virgil*
Serena	*Sheila*
Butterfingers	*Barbra*
Human Side of the News	
Announcer	*Ben*
Dr. Willow	*Dom*
Miss Heinshlinger	*Barbra & Dom*
Strangers on a Train	*Sheila & Ben, Susan & Kenny*
Water on the Brain	*Dom*
Dream House	*Virgil & Entire Cast*

32

With Kenny Adams

Indian Barbra, with Dom De Luise and Sheila Copelan.

"Minnesota" (with Virgil Curry and Sheila Copelan).

REVIEWS

"One observation to be made without fear of contradiction about *Another Evening with Harry Stoones* is that there is plenty of it. Jeff Harris, creator of the revue, is one of those hosts who insists on stuffing his guests. . . . Quantity, even the ancients knew, does not necessarily mean quality. Not that all of this minor contribution to the Off-Broadway season is lackluster. Here and there it is possible to detect flashes of humor and a point of view. *Dream House*, for instance, the final skit, has a touch of true farce. The tourist agency's rhythmic hymn to *Minnesota* is fun. But too often the sharp satirical edge is missing, along with the authentic comic flare. Frequently during the evening there are lapses of taste as Mr. Harris becomes involved with human functions and homosexuality. . . . *Another Evening with Harry Stoones* is not exactly unbearable if nevertheless none too stimulating."

LEWIS FUNKE,
The New York Times

"In the absence of a marquee above the Gramercy Arts Theater, you might look down around your feet for a clue to the attraction within. There on the sidewalk, the producers have commissioned someone to paint a set of hopscotch squares leading to the entrance. The game is very much in the spirit of the show, which stresses genial child's play at the expense of mature humor. It doesn't look like child's play. A lot of work has gone into *Another Evening with Harry Stoones*, and it is evident where it ought to be evident; in bright settings, clever costumes, witty music and capable performances. No one has taken the easy way out with this revue.

"On the whole, though, the show is callow . . . when it deals with children, and it does too often—in seven sketches—it verges on childishness. When it deals with adults, the material plows but rarely bites the already fallow ground of jokes about psychiatrists, television and rock 'n' roll, turning up routines that are more antic than comic. . . . What's lacking in all of this is an original point of view, and nowhere is that more obvious than in the final sketch . . . the collapse of the house, amusing as it is, resembles the downfall of the show—too orderly to be chaotic, too predictable to be inspired."

JOSEPH MORGENSTERN,
New York Herald Tribune

"A brightly spangled, shiny-new package of talented people came tumbling into town Saturday evening, spilling a real evening's worth of entertainment onto the stage of the Gramercy Arts. . . . Perking you up in your seat with a funny overture that endlessly repeats the few opening bars of "Lover," this revue kids everyone and everything, making few pretensions to take itself seriously. Few reviews of late have been as gleeful as this. To begin with, Jeff Harris' first New York presentation leaves no doubt that the young man will be providing us with first-class entertainment for years to come . . . his sketches, especially one set in the boys' and girls' lockers of a New York vocational high school and another about a youngster's birthday party, build up to riotous proportions.

"The eight performers who dash through the 38 numbers—24 in the first act alone—are talented, with many of them exhilaratingly so. . . . Barbara Streisand has been a fine singer for some time and continues to be one. To repeat, *Harry Stoones* will give you a real evening's worth of entertainment."

MARTIN GOTTFRIED,
Women's Wear Daily

"In the category of unblushing high-jinx is a Peter Pan ballet with Harriet All as the pixie ex machina in a special adaptation of the title role; and a Columbus tableau by Mr. Curry, Mr. Keller and three little Indian girls, the Misses Copelan, Susan Belink and Barbra Streisand. *Dream House*, the grand finale, is a piece of montrous nonsense poking impious fun at happy-ending musicals. This all-cast number starring Mr. Curry and Miss Streisand is outrageous, chaotic and a priceless windup to a delightful evening."

TED MORELLO,
New York World-Telegram and Sun

"Every so often comes a skit or lyric with some promise, and performed with skill by an engaging cast. You may find yourself smiling at a Peter Pan who gets stuck on the flight wires, the incomprehensible talk of a beatnik ordering a meal, an amusing spoof of a Dr. Joyce Brothers showing more neuroses than her letter writers . . . or Barbara Streisand weighing the value of one rich boyfriend against another. But these are a few among the many, and the many is pretty bad."

FRANCES HERRIDGE,
New York Post

"The cast was very young and, with the exception of Miss Sands and a couple of the others, rather amateurish. Their high spirits were so contagious, though, that even the bum blackouts—those in which the ideas had been thoroughly joked about before Mr. Harris got into the business—were not really distressing. I particularly admired Sheila Copelan, Ben Keller, and Barbra Streisand, and I hope that they and Mr. Harris and G. Adam Jordan, who directed the show, will not become permanently discouraged by their tough luck."

EDITH OLIVER,
The New Yorker

"Barbra Streisand is a slim, offbeat, deadpan comedienne with an excellent flair for dropping a dour blackout gag, and she belts across a musical apostrophe to New Jersey with facile intensity."

Variety

"The evening has some invigorating surprises, mostly in the form of Diana Sands, an archetypal off-beatnik. Although no one else is quite strong enough to play with her . . . Barbara Streisand can put across a lyric melody and make fine fun of herself at the same time."

MICHAEL SMITH,
The Village Voice

NOTES

One of Barbra's solos, "Value," was used in her Central Park concert and can be heard on the *A Happening in Central Park* album. Jeff Harris wrote another song on that album, "Marty the Martian," as well as "Sweet Zoo" from *My Name Is Barbra*.

In addition to Barbra, Diana Sands and Dom De Luise, whose names have become household words, several of the other "rare, wildly talented actors" in *Another Evening with Harry Stoones* have gone on to success. Susan Belink changed her name to Susan Belling and is now a soprano with the Metropolitan Opera. Kenny Adams cut several albums under the name Rudy Valentyne. Virgil Curry was on tour in 1973 with Alexis Smith in *Applause*. Ben Keller works as a comedy writer along with Jeff Harris in Hollywood, where they had teamed for TV's *Laugh-In*.

"Oh why is it always Miss Marmelstein?"

The Playbill

CAST

(In Order of Appearance)

Miss Marmelstein	Barbra Streisand
Maurice Pulvermacher	Jack Kruschen
Meyer Bushkin	Ken LeRoy
Harry Bogen	Elliot Gould
Tootsie Maltz	James Hickman
Ruthie Rivkin	Marilyn Cooper
Mrs. Bogen	Lillian Roth
Martha Mills	Sheree North
Mario	William Reilly
Mitzi	Barbara Monte
Eddie	Edward Verso
Blanche Bushkin	Bambi Linn
Teddy Asch	Harold Lang
Buggo	Kelly Brown
Miss Springer	Pat Turner
Velma	Francine Bond
Lenny	William Sumner
Norman	Stanley Simmonds
Manette	Luba Lisa
Gail	Wilma Curley
Rosaline	Marion Feis
Noodle	Jack Murray
Sam	Don Grilley
Moxie	Ed Collins
Sheldon Bushkin	Steve Curry
Edith	Margaret Gathright

CREDITS

Produced by   David Merrick
Book by   Jerome Weidman
Based on his novel
Music and lyrics by   Harold Rome
Musical staging by   Herbert Ross
Settings and lighting by   Will Steven Armstrong
Costumes by   Theoni V. Aldredge
Musical direction and vocal arrangements by
Lehman Engel
Orchestrations by   Sid Ramin
Dance and incidental music arranged by   Peter Howard
Production supervised by   Neil Hartley
Directed by   Arthur Laurents

Opened March 22, 1962, at the Sam S. Shubert Theatre

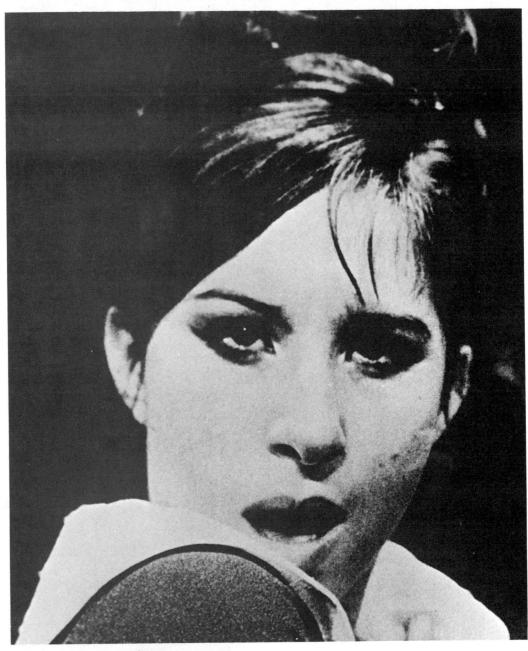

"Miss Marmelstein"

With Elliot Gould and Jack Kruschen

Rehearsing with Elliot Gould and Jack Kruschen

SYNOPSIS

ACT I

With Ken LeRoy

In New York's garment district in 1937, dress manufacturer Maurice Pulvermacher (Jack Kruschen) attempts to cope with a strike of shipping clerks against his firm. His overworked secretary, Miss Marmelstein (Barbra Streisand), tries to cope with him and his problems ("I'm Not a Well Man"). In the midst of all this confusion, in walks one of the strikers, a brash, self-assured young man, Harry Bogen (Elliot Gould). Harry tells the boss that he has a solution to the strike: fire the other strikers and hire Harry's firm, the Needle Trades Delivery Service. Trying to save his business from ruin, Pulvermacher reluctantly signs the contract.

Exultant, Harry shows the contract to his "partner" Tootsie (James Hickman), who reminds him that no such company exists. Harry says they'll just have to borrow money to form the company. He tells Tootsie that nothing will stand in his way—he's tired of being poor ("The Way Things Are"). To get the money he needs, Harry visits his sometime girl friend Ruthie (Marilyn Cooper). Ruthie loves Harry deeply ("When Gemini Meets Capricorn"), but Harry has come for only one purpose—and he succeeds in wooing from Ruthie the capital he needs. He returns home and tells his mother of his new business. As the business grows, he showers her with gifts ("Momma, Momma") and Mrs. Bogen (Lillian Roth) is delighted at her son's ascent from shipping clerk to businessman. Soon, with his shipping business thriving, Harry announces that he is forming his own dress company, Apex Modes, Inc.

Harry begins dating Broadway showgirl Martha Mills (Sheree North). They find that each craves money as much as the other, and they get along famously ("The Sound of Money"). Harry entices two of the best men in the garment trade, Meyer Bushkin (Ken LeRoy) and Teddy Asch (Harold Lang), to leave Pulvermacher and join him in the formation of Apex Modes ("The Family Way"). Later, Ruthie tells Harry's mother that she expects him to propose, but Mrs. Bogen tells her to be patient ("Too Soon"). Ruthie attempts to lure Harry into marriage by mentioning the ten thousand dollar dowry which her husband will get from her father ("Who Knows?"). Normally, this would interest Harry a great deal, but he has just sold out his share of the delivery service, and he has all the money he wants.

In the meantime, Meyer and his wife Blanche (Bambi Linn) express their love for each other ("Have I Told You Lately?") as the first showing of Apex Modes' fashions is arranged for several big wholesale buyers ("Ballad of the Garment Trade"). Martha Mills is the star model, on the Apex payroll at $300.00 per week. The show is a big success and, as the curtain falls on Act I, Harry gives Martha a diamond bracelet and she gives him the key to her apartment.

"What Are They Doing To Us Now?" (with Marilyn Cooper)

BARBRA STREISAND
Miss Marmelstein

Barbra Streisand is nineteen, was born in Madagascar and reared in Rangoon, educated at Erasmus Hall High School in Brooklyn and appeared off Broadway in a one-nighter called *Another Evening with Harry Stoones*. *Wholesale* is her first Broadway show although she has appeared at New York's two best known supper clubs, the Bon Soir and the Blue Angel. She also has appeared eight times on Mike Wallace's PM East and twice on the Paar show. She is not a member of Actors' Studio.

BARBRA STREISAND
Miss Marmelstein

Barbra Streisand is twenty, was born in Zanzibar and reared in Aruba, educated at Erasmus Hall High School in Brooklyn and appeared off Broadway in a one-nighter called *Another Evening with Harry Stoones*. *Wholesale* is her first Broadway show although she has appeared at New York's two best known supper clubs, the Bon Soir and the Blue Angel. She also has appeared eight times on Mike Wallace's PM East and twice on the Paar show.

BARBRA STREISAND
Miss Marmelstein

Barbra Streisand is twenty, was born and reared in Brooklyn, New York, educated at Erasmus Hall High School in Brooklyn and appeared off Broadway in a one-nighter called *Another Evening with Harry Stoones*. *Wholesale* is her first Broadway show although she has appeared at New York's two best known supper clubs, the Bon Soir and the Blue Angel. She also has appeared fifteen times on Mike Wallace's PM, twice on the Paar show and recently on the Garry Moore Show.

ACT II

Harry moves into a penthouse apartment, and begin to spend money lavishly. When Meyer's son receives hi. Bar Mitzvah, Harry presents him with a check to cover his college tuition ("A Gift Today"). Rather than being pleased, Meyer and Teddy suspect that Harry is using company funds for his personal expenses. When they confront Harry with this, he blames it on Miss Marmelstein (who has also joined Apex), saying she mistakenly drew his checks on the company's accounts. Teddy doesn't believe this, and calls Harry a crook. He resolve to audit the company's books and discover the truth.

Back at the office, Miss Marmelstein laments her anonymity ("Miss Marmelstein"). Why doesn't anyone ever call her boobala or Passion Pie? Why is it always jɛ Miss Marmelstein!

Teddy's study of the company's books reveals the f extent of Harry's misuse of company money. He insists that from now on only he, and not Harry, will sign the company checks. Harry fights this, and Meyer gullibly stands by him. Ted quits the partnership, and Harry giv him an I.O.U. for his share. Harry then talks Meyer int opening a new account in Meyer's name ("just to show my honesty"), and he continues to milk the company's coffers. Miss Marmelstein soon warns Meyer that the accounts are in bad shape, and Ruthie tells Harry that tʰ lawyer she works for has been hired by his creditors to collect. She also informs Harry that her boss has propos to her ("A Funny Thing Happened"), but he is unmove With Harry in trouble, Martha latches on to Ted ("What's in it for Me?"). Finally, Apex Modes and Harry are forced into bankruptcy ("What Are They Doing to Us Now?").

Acting the innocent, Harry tells his mother that Meyer may go to jail for the misuse of the company money. Her main concern is that he sit down to a good meal ("Eat a Little Something"). She implores him to dc something to help Meyer, and he finally decides, after much prodding, to go to Meyer's aid. He visits his form boss, Mr. Pulvermacher, and pressures him into putting the money to get Meyer out of jail. He not only gets money, but his job back as well.

With things now looking up again, Harry decides r make one more investment. He accepts Ruthie's marriag proposal, and looks forward to her father's ten thousand dollar dowry.

Barbra's capsule biographies in *Playbill* were producti in themselves. At first the magazine balked at printing w it considered nonsense, but they consented upon Barb. insistence. Not content to leave well enough alone, Bar changed the facts two months later. Not until three mon after the show opened did Barbra's biography reveal true birthplace.

The Bar Mitzvah (with Cast)   *"Miss Marmelstein"*

With Jack Kruschen and Elliot Gould

"Miss Marmelstein"

44

REVIEWS

"Momma, momma, momma, what a good, solid show (the phrase is courtesy of one of Harold Rome's lyrics, the show is *I Can Get It For You Wholesale*, which you can get retail at the Schubert).

"It is unbelievable how much that is touching can come from a show that is essentially tough. Jerome Weidman has not only adapted his novel about a 'Seventh Avenue robber baron' for the musical stage, he has, lo and behold, respected it. His hero is a lout his own mother can scarcely love, his hero's heart lifts only at the lovely 'sound of money,' and the Bronx boys and girls this go-getter betrays for a buck are as real as the tape-measure slung around their necks and the pencils stuck in their hair.

"[Herbert Ross's] energies are put to highly imaginative use ... in two songs Mr. Ross has staged for a sloe-eyed creature with folding ankles named Barbra Streisand (yes, Barbra is spelled right, and Barbra is great).

"Any hesitations? Very few. Heel Elliot Gould performs his chores splendidly ... but what counts is the economy, the speed, the straightforwardness, and the unblinking vigor with which a highly original project, with a great amount of stick-to-itiveness, keeps its vision clear, its head and toes high, and both its musical and dramatic intentions honor-bright."

WALTER KERR,
New York Herald Tribune

"*I Can Get It For You Wholesale* ... could have been called *How to Almost Succeed in Business Without Really Being Honest, or Very Amusing, Either, for That Matter.*

"For it has as its hero a young man with the same insatiable drive as the Machiavellian Mr. Morse of the big hit around the corner, but the trouble is he doesn't have the same charm or ingenuity, and hence he doesn't really succeed. Perhaps, in fact, *Wholesale* would seem better if *Business* hadn't stuck such a lethal pin in the balloon of ambition in industry.

"Elliot Gould, recently promoted from the chorus of *Irma La Douce*, looks and performs skillfully. ... Barbra Streisand, who plays a secretary and resembles an amiable anteater, has her moment in the sun with 'Miss Marmelstein.'"

JOHN McLAIN,
New York Journal-American

"The evening's find is Barbra Streisand, a girl with an oafish expression, a loud, irascible voice and an arpeggiated laugh. Miss Streisand is a natural comedienne, and Mr. Rome has given her a brash, amusing song, 'Miss Marmelstein,' to lament her secretarial fate."

HOWARD TAUBMAN,
The New York Times

"This musical remake of the Jerome Weidman novel is better than the usual pallid fare. Unfortunately, this saga of garment-district chicanery has distinction only part of the time. Its chief virtue is Harold Rome's pungent score. Mr. Rome, of *Pins and Needles* garlands, has composed his best music and penned his best lyrics in years. They have a Thirties bite, a tough, passionate, cynical urban quality. ... The cast is excellent: Lillian Roth, in marvelous voice; Barbra Streisand, a stunning new comic, deft singers-dancers-actors Elliot Gould, Harold Lang, Ken LeRoy; Marilyn Cooper, with a rich vibrant tone; Bambi Linn, a wonderfully expressive dancer. Go."

EMORY LEWIS,
Cue

"In the main the characters are down, down, down. ... I couldn't find one to whom I could give either affection or admiration.

"Well, I guess there was one—but she is a minor mouse in the story. She's a harried, frantic, put-upon, homely frump of a secretary, and she is hilariously played by a 19-year-old newcomer to Broadway, Barbara Streisand. Rome has given her a couple of his jolliest numbers, 'Miss Marmelstein' and 'What Are They Doing to Us Now?'"

JOHN CHAPMAN,
New York Daily News

"Especially to be noted ... a shriek-voiced new comedienne who probably won't be out of work for the next eight years. Her name is Barbra Streisand, who is 19 years old and has packed 38 years of poise and professionalism into her still young life. Miss Streisand, singing or talking, burbling or walking, screaming or whispering, is a great, good friend to *I Can Get It For You Wholesale*"

WHITNEY BOLTON,
New York Morning Telegraph

"... Stimulating is Barbra Streisand, who makes Miss Marmelstein, the secretary-factotum, a being all good nature and exacerbation. Miss Streisand possesses nothing short of a Chekhovian brand of heartbreaking merriment. Gifted with a face that shuttles between those of a tremulous young borzoi and a fatigued Talmudic scholar, and a body that, by way of protective mimesis, has assumed the shape of any other neatly sharpened pencil, she can also sing the lament of the unreconstructed drudge with the clarion peal of an Unliberty Bell."

JOHN SIMON,
Theatre Arts

"Cornet Man"

CAST
(In Order of Appearance)

Fanny Brice	Barbra Streisand
John, Stage Manager	Robert Howard
Emma	Royce Wallace
Mrs. Brice	Kay Medford
Mrs. Strakosh	Jean Stapleton
Mrs. Meeker	Lydia S. Fredericks

I'm The Greatest Star

Winter Garden

PLAYBILL
the magazine for theatregoers

FUNNY GIRL

JUN 1 4 1964

Opening night Playbill—Barbra and Sydney Chaplin

Mrs. O'Malley	Joyce O'Neil
Tom Keeney	Joseph Macaulay
Eddie Ryan	Danny Meehan
Heckie	Victor R. Helou
Workmen	Robert Howard, Robert Henson
Snub Taylor	Buzz Miller
Trombone Smitty	Blair Hammond
Five Finger Finney	Alan E. Weeks
Trumpet Soloist	Dick Perry
Bubbles	Shellie Farrell
Polly	Joan Lowe
Maude	Ellen Halpin
Nick Arnstein	Sydney Chaplin
Two Showgirls	Sharon Vaughn, Diana Lee Nielsen
Stage Director	Marc Jordan
Florenz Ziegfeld, Jr.	Roger DeKoven
Mimsey	Sharon Vaughn
Ziegfeld Tenor	John Lankston
Ziegfeld Lead Dancer	George Reeder
Adolph	John Lankston
Mrs. Nadler	Rose Randolf
Paul	Larry Fuller
Cathy	Joan Cory
Vera	Lainie Kazan
Jenny	Diane Coupe
Ben	Buzz Miller
Mr. Renaldi	Marc Jordan

Showgirls: Prudence Adams, Joan Cory, Diane Coupe, Lainie Kazan, Diane Lee Nielsen, Sharon Vaughn, Rosemarie Yellen.

Singers: Lydia S. Fredericks, Mary Louise, Jeanne McLaren, Joyce O'Neill, Rose Randolf, Stephanie Reynolds, Victor R. Helou, Robert Henson, Robert Howard, Marc Jordan, John Lankston, Albert Zimmerman.

Dancers: Edie Cowan, Christine Dalsey, Shellie Farrell, Ellen Halpin, Rosemary Jelincic, Karen Kristin, Joan Lowe, Robert Avian, Bud Fleming, Larry Fuller, Blair Hammond, John Nola, Alan Peterson, Alan E. Weeks.

Standbys for Miss Streisand and Mr. Chaplin: Lainie Kazan and George Reeder.

CREDITS

Presented by   Ray Stark
Music by   Jule Styne
Lyrics by   Bob Merrill
Book by   Isobel Lennart
Based on her original story.
Musical numbers staged by   Carol Haney
Scenery and lighting by   Robert Randolph
Costumes designed by   Irene Sharaff
Musical direction by   Milton Rosenstock
Orchestrations by   Ralph Burns
Vocal arrangements by   Buster Davis
Dance orchestrations by   Luther Henderson
Associate producer   Lawrence Kasha
Presented in association with   Seven Arts Productions
Production supervised by   Jerome Robbins
Directed by   Garson Kanin

Opened March 26, 1964, at the Winter Garden Theatre

With Sydney Chaplin and Jean Stapleton

SYNOPSIS

ACT I

Backstage at the New Amsterdam Theater, the reigning Ziegfeld Follies star, Fanny Brice (Barbra Streisand), sits before her dressing room mirror. She is awaiting the return of her husband, Nick Arnstein (Sydney Chaplin), after his eighteen months in prison. She knows that they will soon have to make a decision about their future life together. As she reflects on her problems, she recalls her rise to stardom.

She remembers herself as an awkward, unattractive girl, fiercely determined to succeed in show business despite discouragement from her mother's friends ("If a Girl Isn't Pretty"). Befriending Broadway dancer Eddie Ryan (Danny Meehan), Fanny practices with him every day ("I'm the Greatest Star") and is finally given a chance in a ragtime number at Keeney's Music Hall ("Cornet Man"). She is a big hit, and among those who come backstage to congratulate her is Nicky Arnstein (Sydney

Chaplin), who had come to the Music Hall to repay a gambling debt to Keeney (Joseph Macaulay). Fanny is infatuated with the sophisticated Arnstein, but has little time to pine over him, since Florenz Ziegfeld (Roger De Koven) has offered her a spot in his new Follies. Back at her mother's house, Mrs. Brice (Kay Medford) and Eddie congratulate each other for their part in Fanny's success ("Who Taught Her Everything?").

Ziegfeld wants Fanny to appear in an elaborate bridal number ("His Love Makes Me Beautiful"). Unknown to him, Fanny proceeds to play the number for laughs, appearing hugely pregnant during the performance. Ziegfeld is furious, but the gambit wows the audience, and Fanny is hailed as a brilliant new comedienne. Again backstage to offer congratulations is Arnstein, who accepts Fanny's offer to attend her mother's opening night party for her on Henry Street ("I Want to Be Seen With You

"Cornet Man"

Tonight"). At the party ("Henry Street"), Nick and
Fanny feel themselves drawn to each other because of
their mutual need for companionship ("People"). But
Arnstein must leave for a horse farm he has purchased in
Kentucky. Months later, they meet again in Baltimore, and
they have a private dinner at which Nick professes his
love and desire for Fanny ("You Are Woman"). Scheduled to go to Chicago with the Follies, Fanny decides
instead to quit the tour and follow Nick to New York.
Despite the admonishments of her friends, she feels that
this is her one chance for happiness ("Don't Rain on My
Parade"). In New York, Nick and Fanny are married.

"Don't Rain on My Parade"

ACT II

After Fanny and Nick move into a mansion on Long Island, their friends throw a party to welcome them home ("Sadie, Sadie"). Later, in Mrs. Brice's house, Eddie and neighbor Mrs. Strakosh (Jean Stapleton) try to convince Fanny's mother to get married again, now that her daughter is successful ("Find Yourself a Man").

During Fanny's rehearsals for a new Follies, Nick asks Ziegfeld for capital to build a new gambling casino in Florida. Ziegfeld refuses, but Fanny insists on putting up the money. She then begins preparations for a rousing military number in the new show ("Rat-tat-tat-tat"), confident that Nick will soon have a profitable operation. Her opening night is spoiled, however, when her husband fails to appear for it. When he does show up later, he informs her that the casino has failed, and all her money is lost. Fanny makes light of it, hoping to make Nick feel better, but his pride is hurt and he accuses her of treating

him like a child. Fanny begins to have doubts about their relationship ("Who Are You Now?").

Several weeks later, Fanny tries to help Nick get back on his feet by secretly financing a talent agency in order that he be made a partner. Nick discovers what Fanny has done, and is furious that he has become so dependent on his wife. Desperate to salvage some self-respect, he gets involved in an illegal bond deal. Before long, he is arrested for embezzlement. Mrs. Brice makes Fanny realize that much of what has happened is her own fault. Fanny can only think of how much she loves Nick ("The Music That Makes Me Dance").

The final scene is a continuation of the play's opening. Nick, out of prison, tells Fanny that their marriage cannot work. Fanny agrees, and they part. Griefstricken, Fanny refuses to let her sorrow overcome her, and resolves to let her life go on ("Don't Rain on My Parade—Reprise").

"Sadie, Sadie" (with Roger de Koven, Kay Medford and Johnny Desmond)

"You Are Woman, I Am Man"

With Jean Stapleton and Sydney Chaplin

REVIEWS

"Magnificent, sublime, radiant, extraordinary, electric—what puny little adjectives to describe Barbra Streisand. After all, she is merely the most talented performer on the musical comedy stage in the 1960s. In this somewhat abridged and glossy version of Fanny Brice's early years and marriage to Nicky Arnstein, Miss Streisand creates, in cumulative scene after scene, an absolutely believable, intimate portrait of an awkward, chip-on-shoulder, determined girl from Henry Street in love with the stage. Fierce reality is rare in our tinselly musical-comedy theatre. Suddenly at this opening all the false glamour, all the fake trappings fall aside—and real glamour takes over—the glamour of talent. . . . Luckily, this singer-actress does not work in a vacuum. *Funny Girl* is a good show. The first act is the best first act of a musical since *The Black Crook.* . . . You may have guessed by now that I liked *Funny Girl.* Liked? Hell, I loved it."

EMORY LEWIS,
Cue

"Everybody knew Barbra Streisand would be a sta and so she is. Perhaps what is most starlike about her is small thing she does toward the very end of the evenin Sydney Chaplin, as the born gambler who has loved he married her, and then left her to serve a prison sentenc returns. She wants him back. She is ready to sacrifice an thing to have him back. But he—however politely, hov ever kindly, is through, thank you.

"In half a sentence Miss Streisand has dropped h yearning, has dropped the maturity she has been stru gling toward through the entire second act, and is a k again—a defensive kid, a bragging kid, a kidding kid wh won't show she cares. In that half-sentence switch she sue denly summons back for you the whole spindly, ganglin gawking street-angel and stage-angel she has acted out brilliantly in Act One.

"If this emphasis upon the girl who simply devou Act One seems to suggest that Act Two isn't quite in that's right. Act Two isn't a serious letdown, not seriou

"Rat-tat-tat-tat"

"His Love Makes Me Beauti

With Lee Allen

"... Miss Streisand as Fanny hamming it up in her first rendezvous with Sydney Chaplin in a private room in a swank restaurant is almost as funny as the funny girl herself might have been. She uses a fan with mock coyness; she arranges herself on a chair like a rachitic femme fatale; she walks across the room with a wiggle Mae West would envy. These maneuvers nevertheless to a Brice or a Streisand are the small tricks of the clown's trade. What makes Miss Streisand's manipulation of them in this scene particularly impressive is that she conveys a note of honest emotion underneath the clowning."

HOWARD TAUBMAN,
The New York Times

"... Barbra Streisand ... is talent, total, complete, utter and practicing. Vast talent, the kind that comes once in many years. That talent in *Funny Girl* flares and shimmers. Miss Streisand is no pretty girl, no merely pretty girl. She does not need to be and never will. That talent will flame for a long time. Much longer than the vapid accident of beauty."

WHITNEY BOLTON,
New York Morning Telegraph

"Hail to thee, Barbra Streisand; Fanny Brice thou never wert! And there you have the paradox of this show —one spectacular talent in the role of another spectacular talent, but never becoming, or perhaps even trying to become, the woman the play is about. I cannot understand this conceit, or whatever it is, which says an actress must not imitate another actress. In a play about Fanny Brice, she'd better imitate, and do a good job of it. Her job is to recall a personality, not create a new one. Well, for reasons of her own, Miss Streisand prefers to create a 1918 Barbra Streisand, and the justification is that she does it superbly."

NORMAN NADEL,
New York World-Telegram and Sun

"As it turns out, Miss Streisand is all that the preliminary build-up indicated. She's an impressive, versatile talent who clearly has a big future on Broadway and, in the right parts, could also be a bet for pictures—when the cycle turns and the screen is again ready to do musicals."
Variety

enough to make you thoroughly reconsider, but it's thinner than it should be—with the musical numbers taking off into left field—and dry where it shouldn't be.

"One other reservation must be entered. Miss Streisand is pretty much alone now, which means that she carries five of the six second-act numbers. The returns have got to diminish. The star's passion has many colors, her phrasing has many colors, but her voice does not have *that* many. One feels that the management is trying to cram an entire career into one show ... inspiration wanes and craft must make do in its place. Still, it's the star's evening; long may she wave to Mr. Ziegfeld. The show as a whole, considering its tendency to lose weight, can't be called a clean knockout. Suppose we settle for a TKO."

WALTER KERR,
New York Herald Tribune

"Yes, Barbra Streisand is all they've said she is, and fairly often in *Funny Girl* she finds opportunities to do her stuff. As a performer she represents a remarkable and rare meeting between a common touch that leads us all to identify with her and a show business sheen that makes her our ideal. When both are going at once, the effect is thrilling. *Funny Girl* is a perfunctory musical with, sans Streisand anyway, not much reason for being. The story of Fanny Brice is too simple to make a real plot, and its few possibilities for conflict are left wholly unexplored."
The Village Voice

NOTES

Barbra was nominated for a Tony Award as Best Actress in a Musical, but she lost the award to Carol Channing in *Hello, Dolly!* In 1965, she was crowned "Miss Ziegfeld" by the Ziegfeld Club.

In June 1965 Sydney Chaplin was replaced by Johnny Desmond, and Lee Allen took over the Eddie Ryan role. Barbra left the show in December 1965. She was replaced by Mimi Hines, whose husband, Phil Ford, assumed the Eddie Ryan role. The show continued to run a year after Barbra left it.

"Cornet Man"

The Playbill

CAST

(In Order of Appearance)

Fanny Brice	Barbra Streisand
John, Stage Manager	John Griffin
Emma	Isabelle Lucas
Mrs. Brice	Kay Medford
Mrs. Strakosh	Stella Moray
Mrs. Meeker	Frances Wells Robertson
Mrs. O'Malley	Lorraine Quinn
Tom Keeney	Jack Cunningham
Eddie Ryan	Lee Allen
Heckie	Stanley Fleet
Workman	David Wheldon Williams
Snub Taylor	Jimmy Land
Trombone Smitty	Keith Lee
Five Finger Finney	Tony Kemp
Bubbles	Jill Rose
Polly	Delia Sainsbury
Maude	Linda Lawrence
Nick Arnstein	Michael Craig
Two Showgirls	Valerie Leon and Maggie Wright
Stage Director	John Moore
Florenz Ziegfeld, Jr.	Ronald Leigh-Hunt
Mimsey	Maggie Wright
Ziegfeld Tenor	David Wheldon Williams
Ziegfeld Lead Dancer	David Wright
Adolph	David Wheldon Williams
Mrs. Nadler	Eileen Shaw
Paul	David Wright
Actor	Lewis Henry
Cathy	Valerie Leon
Vera	Sarah Brackett
Jenny	Jennie Walton
Mr. Renaldi	Stanley Fleet

Showgirls: Sarah Brackett, Jane Clarke, Valerie Leon, Melvina Price, Jennie Walton, Maggie Wright.

Singers: Susan Hardy, Virginia Hudson, Diana Landor, Lorraine Quinn, Frances Wells Robertson, Eileen Shaw, Stanley Fleet, Lewis Henry, John Griffin, John Moore, Stephen Taylor, David Wheldon Williams.

Dancers: Heather Clifton, Elizabeth Edmiston, Linda Lawrence, Jill Rose, Delia Sainsbury, Rosemary Smith, Chris Blackwell, Ian Kaye, Tony Kemp, Jimmy Land, Maurice Lane, Keith Lee, Johnny Shack, David Wright.

CREDITS

New York Production credits apply, with these exceptions: Presented by Bernard Delfont and Arthur Lewis. Choreographed by Larry Fuller. Musical direction by Marcus Dods. Directed by Lawrence Kasha.

Opened April 13, 1966, at the Prince of Wales Theatre

With Michael Craig

"Rat-tat-tat-tat"

REVIEWS

"It would be an exaggeration to say that the only reason for seeing this thunderously publicized show is the redeeming presence of Barbra Streisand. But it is also true that Miss Streisand makes one temporarily accept one of the most nonsensical plots in the history of the American musical.

"As this is the first time she has appeared in this country, it is hard to decide whether she is acting the role or simply being herself. She certainly has technical blindspots. Playing anything but comedy she is dull; and often, in dialogue as well as lyrics, she becomes inaudible. What she does project is the same force of personality which must have carried Fanny Brice to the top."

The Times (London)

"Sadie, Sadie" (with Kay Medford and Michael Craig)

"Sadie, Sadie" (with Chorus)

"Miss Streisand has a neat, pocket-size humor, expressing itself in small, mocking gestures, and alarming fingernails that would interest a vampire. The battery of microphones enables the front rows to hear her when she speaks, and the back when she sings. The rich and leisured can thus get the entire show at two visits if they arrange their seats properly. Or they could if the show were not almost entirely sold out for the 14 weeks during which Miss Streisand is contracted to appear in it."

HAROLD HOBSON,
The London Sunday Times

"For the next 14 weeks, people who visit the Prince of Wales won't be going to a theatre. They'll be making a pilgrimage to a shrine. There, a goddess called Barbra Streisand makes every song she sings sound like a hymn and rouses her audiences to ecstacy."

JACK LEWIS,
The Sunday Citizen

"Barbra Streisand in *Funny Girl* . . . is a prodigious and unique creature—a kind of guardian demon of show-biz, the only three-dimensional strip-cartoon heroine in existence. Her personality is that of a ten-year-old girl show-off, teetering in her mother's high heels and camping in her old evening dress, enjoying her own pretense of fooling us that she is grown-up."

The Sunday Telegraph

"The show is Barbra Streisand. Take away this pulsating dynamo with the 1,000-volt voice and there would not be enough glow left to light up your programme. She is the heart, the soul, the sound and the music. Without her, *Funny Girl*—for all its folksy humour, gaudy display and schmaltzy fun from a rasping but scintillating 'Yiddisher Momma'—would be as forlorn as sausage denied of its mash . . . if those magical vocal cords and that insolently sexy frame should temporarily be indisposed, my heart would bleed for the palpitating understudy. . . . Whether she is up there staggering around in blue bloomers or sagging-kneed and spindly-legged or sliding seductively on a vermilion chaise-longue, she looks as edible and as enticing as a plate of hot pastrami."

DONALD ZEC,
Daily Mirror

"She sings, and there are saxophones and trumpets and violins in her throat. Her voice takes off on smooth gravel, and soars about in some previously uncharted musical magic land of sweetness."

Daily Sketch

"The question has been asked, 'Is it possible that Barbra Streisand is overrated?'. Of course it's possible, and considering the amount of publicity injected into *Funny Girl* it was even probable. Her talents are small, but at least it can be said, for a start, that when it comes to belting out a song she can do it in the best Broadway style, with undertones of Brooklyn and even of Jersey City. Although overrated she seems bound to prove irresistible to the uncritical."

GERARD FAY,
The Guardian

With Michael Craig

NOTES

Barbra's performance in *Funny Girl* took London by storm. She was voted the Best Foreign Actress and *Funny Girl* was named Best Foreign Musical. The show's title was soon to become as much associated with Barbra as with Fanny Brice. When Barbra and Elliot announced in London that Barbra was expecting their first child, and she would have to cancel $1 million in concert tours, New York's *Daily News* headlined the story "Million $ Baby for 'Funny Girl.' "

BARBRA IN LONDON

Arriving at London's Heathrow airport.

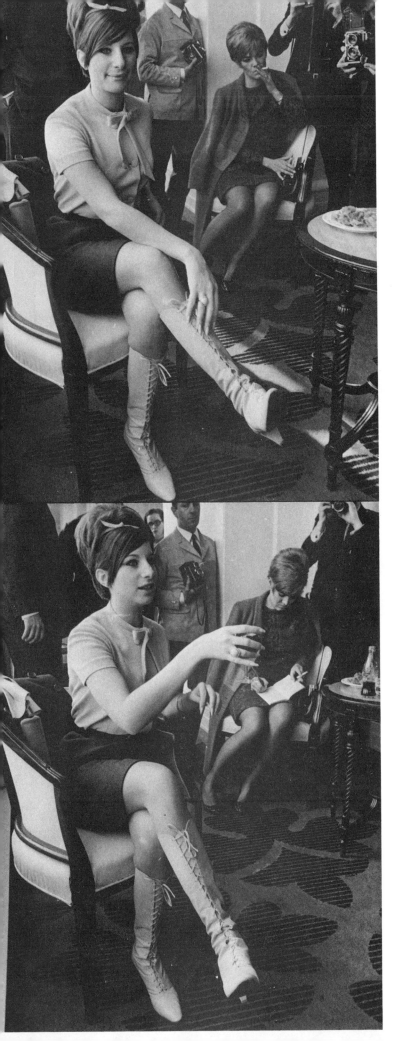

Meeting the Press in London

On her way to the theatre

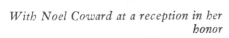

With Noel Coward at a reception in her honor

Barbra meets Princess Margaret

Barbra and Goddard Lieberson, President of Columbia Records, sign her first recording contract in 1963

Whatever else Barbra Streisand may have done or may do, most people still consider her first and foremost a singer. And with good reason. It was her voice which opened the show business doors for her. It is an awesome instrument of power, beauty and purity. Her voice is the best of any popular singer, past or present, and she has, to go along with that voice, a unique understanding of her material and an uncanny instinct for interpretation.

Since 1963 she has been the most popular female vocalist in the world. Her recordings have earned dozens of Gold Record Awards, and she has three personal Grammys. When she first started out, however, her potential for widespread popular appeal wasn't too highly regarded. . . .

The first recording of Barbra Streisand's voice appeared on the Columbia Records Original Cast Album of *I Can Get It For You Wholesale*. Her show-stopper, "Miss Marmelstein," is immortalized on that recording, and her brilliantly comic performance of this number is one of the few memorable moments in a largely forgettable score.

Almost simultaneously, Barbra sang on another Columbia LP, the 25th Anniversary Edition of another Harold Rome musical, *Pins and Needles*, which, by further coincidence, was also about the New York garment center. Barbra was asked to audition for this album at the suggestion of Miles Kreuger, then a producer at Columbia and now head of the Institute of the American Musical. "I had seen Barbra at the Lion," Kreuger remembers, "and I thought she'd be perfect for the songs on this album."

Pins and Needles contains a series of delightful tunes about unions and the life of the working class. Barbra sings six of these, including three satirical put-downs, "Sitting on Your Status Quo," "Doing the Reactionary" and "Not Cricket to Picket"; a lack-of-love song, "What Good Is Love," sung in a sullen downbeat with a hint of music hall honky-tonk; and her most memorable effort, "Nobody Makes a Pass at Me." Similar to "Miss Marmelstein," it is the lament of an unloved and unlovely girl who remains alone despite her use of all the best products on the market. The song, plaintively intoned in Barbra's inimitable deadpan style, ends in a miserable, whining "I don't know . . . oh, dear . . ." which tugs at our heartstrings while breaking us up.

It was Barbra's work on these two albums which convinced Columbia that they should put her under contract. She was asked to audition for Columbia's president, Goddard Lieberson, and she remembers he was a little skeptical: "He said I wouldn't sell records, that I was much too special, that I would appeal only to a small clique who would dig me." But Lieberson decided to go with Streisand anyway, and the rest is history: "The first album went right on the charts," says Barbra. "And the second one too. Everyone was surprised. But I always knew it would happen this way. People were ready for me."

The Barbra Streisand Album, released in March 1963, was an exciting collection of the songs Streisand had introduced at the Lion, Bon Soir and Blue Angel—beautiful ballads languidly sung, outrageous ditties laughingly performed and old standards with a new twist. People across the country were as taken with Barbra's beautiful voice, vibrant talent and unique material as her nightclub audiences had been. Her melancholy rendition of the usually up-tempo Democratic Party theme "Happy Days Are Here Again" created a sensation and became a best-selling single. Altogether, the album was a milestone in recording history. It was chosen as "Album of the Year" by the Academy of Recording Arts and Sci-

Recording The Barbra Streisand Album

nces at its 1964 Grammy Awards, and Barbra won a Grammy for "Best
emale Vocal Performance" for "Happy Days." Harold Arlen's liner
otes for the record's jacket have proven prophetic: "I advise you to
atch Barbra Streisand's career. This young lady (a mere twenty), has a
unning future. Keep listening, keep watching. And please remember, I
ld you so. . . ."

The Second Barbra Streisand Album, released in August, was pri-
arily a collection of love songs which Barbra delivered as strong per-
onal statements. She performs "Any Place I Hang My Hat Is Home"
ith such intensity that one believes she is living, not merely singing, the
rics. This album enhanced Barbra's reputation as a highly emotional
erformer.

Barbra's third album (called, surprisingly, *The Third Album*) had a
omewhat different personality than her first two. It contains no innova-
ons, no comedy and very little strong emotion. The melodic songs are,
or the most part, mellow and reflective, making for what is termed in
cording parlance "easy listening."

Columbia "lent" Barbra to Capitol Records for her next album, the
riginal cast recording of *Funny Girl*. This disc preserves Barbra's
xciting performance in that show, and contains her original versions of
ich favorites as "People," "Don't Rain on My Parade" and "I'm the
reatest Star." It also contains, and is most valuable for, the songs which
eren't used in the film version of the play: "I Want to Be Seen With
ou Tonight," "Rat-tat-tat-tat," "Who Are You Now?" and two of the
est numbers in the score, "Cornet Man" and "The Music That Makes Me
ance."

This album won a Grammy Award for "Best Score from an Original
ast Show Album" and was nominated as "Album of the Year" for 1964
losing out to *The Barbra Streisand Album*).

Barbra's recording of this album typifies such sessions. Unsatisfied
ith the first tape, she insisted it be done over until she thought it perfect.
he session continued late into the night. On the monophonic version,
hich was recorded after the stereo, Barbra can be heard, at the height of
e rag-tag number "Cornet Man," shouting, "We're going home!"—her
ue to her overworked musicians that the end was in sight.

A collection of unusual and provocative songs comprised Barbra's
ext album, *People*, named for and including a new version of the popular
allad from *Funny Girl*. Her voice, as indicated on this disc, was
nproving all the time, and it was clear that she was far more than a show
usiness flash-in-the-pan. This album won Barbra her second Grammy as
Best Female Vocalist." Peter Matz was honored by the Recording
cademy for his accompaniment and Don Bronstein's photo was chosen
Best Album Cover."

A single version of the "People" cut was released and became a
est-seller and a song closely associated with Barbra Streisand. It was
ominated for Grammy Awards as both "Song of the Year" and "Record
f the Year." The *People* album was nominated as "Album of the Year."

People quickly shot up to the Number 1 best-selling position on the
ashbox "Top 100 LPs" list. During one week in October of 1964, no
wer than five Streisand recordings (her first four solo LPs and the
unny Girl disc) were in the top 100. Barbra requested a copy of that
eek's chart, and it adorned a wall of her New York apartment, along
ith several Gold Records which those albums had earned.

Barbra's success in television was soon reflected in her recordings as

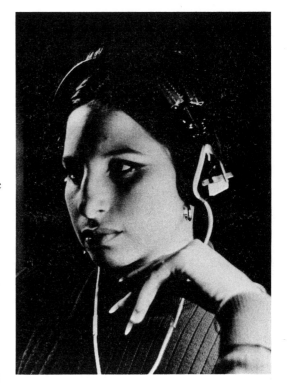

Listening to a playback of Funny Girl

Barbra at two recording sessions during the mid-sixties

soundtrack albums of her specials were released. Her first show resulted in two LPs, *My Name Is Barbra* and *My Name is Barbra, Two.* These contain many of the songs Barbra sang on television, plus several new numbers. Among these were "Jenny Rebecca," "My Pa" and "I've Got No Strings," which added to the first album's mood and made fine substitutes for the songs Barbra had previously recorded. *My Name Is Barbra* won Streisand her third straight Grammy and received nominations for "Album of the Year" and for "Best Album Cover" (Sheldon Streisand's photo of his little sister).

Color Me Barbra again captured the excitement of a Streisand special, although some of the magic was lost without the accompaniment of the elaborate production numbers of the show. The album's cover, a charming sketch, was inspired by "Draw Me a Circle" on *The Third Album.* Color Me Barbra won Grammy nominations as "Album of the Year" and for Barbra, "Best Female Vocal Performance."

Barbra's next album was her first radical departure from the type of material she had performed in her first seven solo albums. *Je m'appelle Barbra* was the star's only attempt at recording a collection of French songs, both in English and French versions. (The first song she had ever sung in French, "Non C'est Rien," appeared on the *Color Me Barbra*

Another People *sitting*

album, perhaps as a preview of what was to come.)

The disc reveals a Barbra with a remarkably good French accent, who sounds very much like Edith Piaf. In fact, as the fascinating liner notes by Nat Shapiro tell us, a song written for Miss Piaf, "I've Been Here" ("Le Mur"), was held back for a year after her death so that Barbra could record it for this album. The English lyrics were written especially for Streisand, and she performs the song in both French and English.

Another milestone for Barbra on this album is her first musical composition, aptly titled "Ma Premiere Chanson," a simple, charming melody with lyrics in French by Eddy Marnay. All in all, *Je m'appelle Barbra* stands as one of her best, and certainly most unusual, efforts.

With *Simply Streisand*, Barbra returned to the American fold with a collection of lilting melodies including "My Funny Valentine," "I'll Know" and "The Boy Next Door" (more American than that you couldn't get!). Included in this album was Barbra's hit single "Stout Hearted Men," performed, in a throwback to "Happy Days," as a slow ballad.

Barbra's next recording wasn't a Barbra Streisand album but a Harold Arlen album. On *Harold Sings Arlen (With Friend)*, Barbra does a lovely

solo version of "House of Flowers" and joins Arlen for a spirited rendition of "Ding Dong the Witch Is Dead" from *The Wizard of Oz*. Reviewing this album in *High Fidelity*, John S. Wilson wrote: "Arlen was one of Miss Streisand's earliest advocates and it is fascinating to discover, as one hears them in duet, that her now familiar singing style is actually very similar to his, particularly in the strong, fully rounded way she projects every aspect of a song."

The album, released in 1966, is out of print and has become an extremely rare collector's item.

It was inevitable that Barbra would eventually release a Christmas album. It happened in 1967, and the disc turned out to be not only one of Barbra's best efforts, but one of the finest seasonal albums ever. Side One is devoted to light holiday ditties, including a tongue-in-cheek version of "Jingle Bells." Side Two contains spiritual songs, and some of Barbra's best singing. *Barbra Streisand/A Christmas Album* is a best-seller each year.

On June 17th, 1967, 135,000 people jammed into New York's Central Park to hear Barbra Streisand give a concert. It was the largest audience ever amassed to see a single performer, and the evening was one of the most memorable in show business history. The two-and-one-half-hour concert was taped and highlights were presented as Barbra's fourth television special. The tape from that show became Barbra's 15th album. *A Happening in Central Park* re-creates the excitement and spontaneity of that evening, and contains some stunning new songs including the beautiful ballad "New Love Is Like a Newborn Child." It also contains one of Barbra's oldest songs, "Value," which stopped the show the night she performed it, six years before, in *Another Evening with Harry Stoones*.

What About Today, released in 1969, was Barbra's first foray into the "today" sound of such composers as John Lennon and Paul McCartney, Buffy St. Marie, Paul Simon and Jim Webb. She molded these songs, most of which had been recorded by others previously, to her own special style and made them her own. The album was highly successful primarily due to its collection of socially relevant, as well as tuneful, songs. Barbra's liner notes commend young people for their involvement in improving the world around them.

The soundtrack album of Barbra's first film, *Funny Girl*, records one of the finest musical comedy performances on film. Barbra's renditions of the songs from the Broadway show were improvements over her original versions, and although several excellent songs were dropped from the score, their replacements were in some cases even better. Barbra singing "I'd Rather Be Blue" is a highlight of the film and the album, and the new title song, "Funny Girl," is a lovely ballad if not quite on a par with the song it usurped, "The Music That Makes Me Dance." Barbra received her first Grammy nomination in three years, as "Best Female Vocalist," for this LP.

Barbra's second soundtrack album, *Hello, Dolly!*, turns out, in the final analysis, to be more enjoyable than the film it represents. While the movie was burdened with a nonsensical plot and unbelievable characters, the album contains only the film's songs, which are pleasant and melodic. Barbra's duet with Louis Armstrong on the title song is especially winning. Several songs were added to the film score, including "Just Leave Everything to Me" and "Love Is Only Love." The latter number was written not for *Hello, Dolly!* but for another Jerry Herman musical, *Mame*. It was dropped from that show during out-of-town tryouts, and Herman, thinking the song suitable to describe Dolly's relationship with Horace Vandergelder, made it a part of the *Dolly* score.

Hello, Dolly! was Barbra's first non-Columbia album since the original cast recording of *Funny Girl*; it was released by 20th Century–Fox records.

Barbra Streisand's Greatest Hits, released early in 1970, contained some of the best cuts from Barbra's previous solo Columbia albums. It is notable on its own primarily for a full-length version of "Sam, You Made the Pants Too Long," only a part of which was used in a medley on *Color Me Barbra*. The albums's cover photo of Barbra, by Lawrence Schiller, is especially attractive.

Barbra's third film, *On a Clear Day You Can See Forever*, afforded her the opportunity to play two roles, look absolutely gorgeous and sing several beautiful Alan Jay Lerner-Burton Lane numbers, including "Love With All The Trimmings," "He Isn't You," "What Did I Have That I Don't Have?" and the title song. Several other songs recorded for the film were not included in the soundtrack. They do, however, appear on a demonstration cut released prior to the film's final editing. Jack Nicholson's movie singing debut wound up on the cutting room floor, but he does a creditable job with a difficult song, "Who Is There Among Us Who Knows?" at the end of which Barbra is heard humming. Another song on the demo album but not in the movie is "Wait 'Til We're Sixty-Five," a playful duet between Barbra and Larry Blyden in which they musically discuss the old-age benefits of Chemical Foods, Inc.

Barbra's first non-singing role in *The Owl and the Pussycat* became her first non-singing LP. The hilarious verbal battles between Barbra and George Segal are preserved for home enjoyment. The album also contains the evocative music of the popular rock group, Blood, Sweat and Tears.

In late 1970, Streisand released a single recording of a rock song, "Stoney End," written by young composer Laura Nyro. Barbra's first such attempt, the record had difficulty being accepted by the top rock radio stations across the country, which rarely had played any Streisand songs. After several months and increasing sales, however, it made its way into the radio land frequented by today's young people, and then it took off. Before long, it was among the top ten best-selling records in the country, the first Streisand single to reach that plateau since "People," a vastly different song, six years before.

Barbra's success with this single caused Columbia to rush into release Barbra's first rock album, pre-empting a scheduled disc containing more traditional music. That album never was released. The rock effort, *Stoney End*, released late in 1971, contained the single as well as other rock and folk songs by new young composers. The LP achieved great success as Barbra proved she could appeal to young people by singing their music while still retaining her own individual style. She released a single cut from the album, "Time and Love," which was not as successful as "Stoney End" but further established Barbra as a "rock singer."

Her next album continued the trend set by *Stoney End*. *Barbra Joan Streisand* featured more songs by such popular young artists as Carole King, Laura Nyro and James Taylor. There were two songs by John Lennon and a Burt Bacharach-Hal David medley, "A House Is Not a Home/One Less Bell to Answer," the high point of the album. In a gesture to the young music fans who were now buying Streisand records more than ever before, the album contained a 22″ × 32″ poster portrait of Barbra.

The front and back covers of *Barbra Joan Streisand* are very curious. Side 1 shows Barbra looking sad. Her name is spelled with one "a" and the bump in her nose has been airbrushed out. Side 2 features a happy, smiling, self-satisfied Barbra, her name spelled as it originally was, with the

bump in her nose back in its full glory. Barbra's desire to "be herself" at this point in time appears to have manifested itself in this album's graphics.

Live Concert at The Forum is only Barbra's second "live" album, recorded at a benefit for Senator George McGovern's Presidential campaign in April 1972. It contains several new Streisand cuts, "Didn't We?" "Sweet Inspiration/Where You Lead" (which won Barbra her sixth Grammy nomination as "Best Female Vocalist") and the charming "Sing" from TV's *Sesame Street*, which Barbra combined to great effect with "Make Your Own Kind of Music." Included with this package is another poster, a reproduction of the cover sketch.

This album catches Barbra's showmanship and the excitement of a live concert, but it is marred by repetition of songs which Streisand has recorded before. By far the worst offender in this regard is "People." This album is the *sixth* on which Barbra sings this song, and no matter how beautiful a song it may be, no matter how much it has come to be Barbra's theme, it can be, and has been, overdone. One can only hope that this will be the last Barbra Streisand album on which it will appear.

Barbra's twenty-fourth album is a recording of most of her fifth television special, *Barbra Streisand . . . And Other Musical Instruments*. It has all the strengths of the program and, unfortunately, all its weaknesses too. Barbra is in fine voice, and she adds some marvelous renditions to her collection—"By Myself," "Johnny One Note" and "Glad to Be Unhappy." She also introduces some new and unusual material—"Auf dem Wasser zu Singen," by Franz Schubert, and "I Never Has Seen Snow," by Harold Arlen and Truman Capote.

Sadly the elements that hurt the show hurt this album too. The conglomeration of sounds produced alternately by foreign instruments, electronic gadgets and household appliances drown Barbra out in many instances and make "easy listening" difficult. The album also contains "People," but Barbra—mercifully—limits it to just one line. It is, ultimately, Barbra's voice and what she does with it on this album that makes it worthwhile.

Whatever the course of her career in other media, Barbra will undoubtedly continue to cut records. Her recording career has been one of boldness, innovation and flexibility. She has made hits out of long-forgotten musical compositions, she has recorded up-tempo numbers in a downbeat and ballads in an upbeat. Recently, she has moved into the contemporary musical genre, adding her own unique stylization to today's music.

Barbra's voice has been said to be "of inestimable benefit to whatever she chooses to sing." Her collection of LPs is one of the most distinguished of any artist in recording history, and her future efforts can only add to her memorable recording career.

With Goddard Lieberson in 1966. Barbra is pregnant with Jason.

CAN GET IT FOR YOU WHOLESALE
(Columbia Original Cast Recording, 1962)

PRODUCED FOR THE STAGE BY DAVID MERRICK.
DIRECTED BY ARTHUR LAURENTS.
MUSICAL DIRECTION AND VOCAL ARRANGEMENTS
BY LEHMAN ENGEL.
MUSIC AND LYRICS BY HAROLD ROME.
ORCHESTRATIONS BY SID RAMIN.
DANCE AND INCIDENTAL MUSIC ARRANGED BY
PETER HOWARD.
ALBUM PRODUCED BY GODDARD LIEBERSON.
NOTES BY CURTIS F. BROWN.

SIDE 1

Overture
I'm Not a Well Man
(Streisand, Kruschen)
The Way Things Are
(Gould)
When Gemini Meets Capricorn
(Cooper, Gould)
Momma, Momma
(Gould, Roth)
The Sound of Money (Gould,
North, Monte, Reilly, Verso)
The Family Way (Roth, Gould,
Cooper, Lang, Linn, LeRoy)
Too Soon
(Roth)
Who Knows?
(Cooper)
Have I Told You Lately?
(LeRoy, Linn)
Ballad of the Garment Trade
(Streisand, Cooper, Linn, Gould,
Lang, LeRoy and Company)

SIDE 2

A Gift Today (Curry, Gould, Roth,
Linn, LeRoy, Cooper)
Miss Marmelstein
(Streisand)
A Funny Thing Happened
(Cooper, Gould)
What's in It For Me?
(Lang, North)
What Are They Doing to Us Now?
(Streisand, Brown, Hickman,
Lisa, Curley, Turner and Chorus)
Eat a Little Something
(Roth, Gould)

REVIEWS

"A standout performance is contributed by Barbra Streisand, an ungainly, even grotesque-looking girl with expressive arms and hands, who in Miss Marmelstein gives an uproariously humorous picture of a harassed secretary striving for efficiency in an organization flooded with incompetents."

JOHN F. INDCOX,
High Fidelity

"Harold Rome has whipped up an in-and-out score for this musical version of Jerome Weidman's novel of New York's garment center. But what's 'in' is good and what's 'out' isn't bad and the original Broadway cast makes the most of it all ... The material showstopper, and a lot of the credit should be given to Barbra Streisand's performance, is 'Miss Marmelstein.' "

Variety

PINS AND NEEDLES
(Columbia, 1962)

TWENTY-FIFTH ANNIVERSARY EDITION OF THE
MUSICAL REVUE.
MUSIC AND LYRICS BY HAROLD ROME.
RECORDING SUPERVISED BY HAROLD ROME.
COVER ART BY ANTONAKOS.
BACK COVER PHOTOS BY HANK PARKER.
MUSICAL DIRECTION BY STAN FREEMAN.
VOCAL ARRANGEMENTS BY ELISE BRETTON.
NOTES BY CHARLES BURR AND DAVID DUBINSKY.
PRODUCED BY ELIZABETH LAUER AND
CHARLES BURR.

SIDE 1

Sing Me a Song With Social
Significance (*Rose Marie Jun*)
Doing the Reactionary
(*Barbra Streisand*)
One Big Union For Two
(*Jack Carroll, Rose Marie Jun*)
It's Better With a Union Man
(*Harold Rome*)
Nobody Makes a Pass at Me
(*Streisand*)
I've Got the Nerve to Be in Love
(*Carroll, Jun*)
Not Cricket to Picket
(*Streisand*)
Back to Work
(*Carroll and Chorus*)

SIDE 2

Status Quo
(*Streisand*)

When I Grow Up
(*Rome*)

Chain Store Daisy
(*Jun*)

Four Little Angels of Peace
(*Rome, Carroll,
Streisand, Alan Sokoloff*)

Sunday in the Park
(*Carroll*)

What Good Is Love?
(*Streisand*)

Mene, Mene Tekel
(*Rome and Chorus*)

REVIEWS

"An historic musical revue has been recreated in this package with a buoyancy of spirit that will delight the showtune collectors and introduce neophytes to an exciting period in the annals of the American stage. . . . In putting the package together, disc producers Elizabeth Lauer and Charles Burr have wisely started with the composer himself, who probably sings Rome better than anyone. In support they've got Barbra Streisand, from Rome's current Broadway tuner *I Can Get It for You Wholesale*, Rose Marie Jun and Jack Carroll. All hands are delightful. . . ."
Variety

". . . 'Nobody Makes a Pass at Me,' the tale of a girl who buys every product guaranteed to enhance feminine appeal but still remains unnoticed is, of course, an ageless lament. The original version of this, . . . sung by Millie Wertz, was, until recently, available on the Decca label, but that rendition is now completely surpassed by a gorgeously funny performance by Barbra Streisand, a genuine comedy find. Here Miss Streisand sounds very much like a young Fanny Brice; again, in 'Not Cricket to Picket,' she sounds surprisingly like Beatrice Lillie."

JOHN F. INDCOX,
High Fidelity

THE BARBRA STREISAND ALBUM
(Columbia, 1963)

PRODUCED BY MIKE BERNIKER.
MUSIC ARRANGED AND CONDUCTED BY PETER MATZ.
COVER PHOTOGRAPH BY HENRY PARKER.
NOTES BY HAROLD ARLEN.

SIDE 1

Cry Me a River
My Honey's Loving Arms
I'll Tell the Man in the Street
A Taste of Honey
Who's Afraid of the Big, Bad Wolf?
Soon It's Gonna Rain

SIDE 2

Happy Days Are Here Again
Keepin' Out of Mischief Now
Much More
Come to the Supermarket (in Old Peking)
A Sleepin' Bee

REVIEWS:

"Barbra Streisand's hilarious performance as Miss Marmelstein in *I Can Get It For You Wholesale* (the highpoint of that otherwise mediocre musical) introduced to Broadway a new female clown of unusual talent. Her comedy style . . . has marked individuality. But as habitues of New York supper clubs know—and as this new Columbia album so positively demonstrates—Miss Streisand has another talent. She is a remarkably accomplished singer of popular Lieder, with a voice of pure and rather unusual timbre which she uses quite brilliantly in a repertoire running all the way from torch ballads and show tunes to novelty numbers."

JOHN F. INDCOX,
High Fidelity

"The eagerly awaited Barbra Streisand album . . . turns out to be a fascinating package. Miss Streisand is a compelling stylist with a full, rich vocal quality that may give you goosebumps when you hear her more dramatic arias. She has a sure control and knows what she is doing at all times. There are few (if any) better versions of 'Cry Me a River' and 'Soon It's Gonna Rain' . . . My only complaint is that the supposedly comic numbers—'Who's Afraid of the Big, Bad Wolf?' and 'Come to the Supermarket in Old Peking'—are out of place in the program; they lose their point when heard away from the situations for which they were created."

STANLEY GREEN,
Hi Fi/Stereo Review

THE SECOND BARBRA STREISAND ALBUM
(Columbia, 1963)

PRODUCED BY MIKE BERNIKER.

ARRANGED AND CONDUCTED BY PETER MATZ.

ADDITIONAL MATERIALS BY PETER DANIELS.

COVER PHOTO BY WOOD KUZOUMI.

LINER NOTES BY JULE STYNE.

SIDE 1

Any Place I Hang My Hat Is Home
Right as the Rain
Down With Love
Who Will Buy?
When the Sun Comes Out

SIDE 2

Gotta Move
My Coloring Book
I Don't Care Much
Lover, Come Back to Me
I Stayed Too Long at the Fair
Like a Straw in the Wind

REVIEWS

"Having been extremely enthusiastic about Barbra Streisand's first album, I find it neither easy nor pleasant to report that her new album seems to me an almost unrelieved bore. I have no idea what has happened to this singer between albums (maybe she took a course in method singing), but her work here is pretentiously arty, overinvolved and overprojected, and made further intolerable by a vocal tone best described by the Irish word

'keening.' There is certainly nothing wrong with her choice of songs, five of which are by Harold Arlen, and there are occasional flashes of the old Streisand . . . her 'Who Will Buy?' from *Oliver!* starts out on the credit side of the ledger, but suddenly, with a lot of wretched phrasings, the whole mood is shattered and never recaptured."

JOHN F. INDCOX,
High Fidelity

"Barbra Streisand's vocal dramatics pulled her first LP effort into the best-selling class and further established her as the foremost young singer on disks. . . . This follow-up will enhance her reputation and bring more coin into the Columbia coffers. She's mostly on a Harold Arlen kick in this songbag . . . Arlen's moody melodies suit her perfectly and she kicks off each one with a potent delivery. Her first single disk, 'My Coloring Book,' didn't do too well in the sales department, but its inclusion here shows that she can really belt a pop item as well."

Variety

THE THIRD ALBUM
(Columbia, 1963)

PRODUCED BY MIKE BERNIKER.
ARRANGED AND CONDUCTED BY RAY ELLIS, SID
RAMIN, PETER DANIELS, PETER MATZ.
COVER PHOTO BY RODDY MCDOWELL.
LINER NOTES BY SAMMY CAHN.

SIDE 1

My Melancholy Baby
Just in Time
Taking a Chance on Love
Bewitched (Bothered and Bewildered)
Never Will I Marry

SIDE 2

As Time Goes By
Draw Me a Circle
It Had to Be You
Make Believe
I Had Myself a True Love

REVIEWS

"Barbra Streisand's third album differs from her first two; its impact is more the kind to sneak up on you than to hit you on the head. But even when Miss Streisand is sneaking, she shows a vocal skill far above that of most singers of popular songs. Because she is geared toward underplaying here she indulges her penchant for stretching out a melodic line just as far as she can take it—a device that is, for the most part, very effective in 'My Melancholy Baby' and 'Bewitched,' although there are moments elsewhere when she stretches things just a bit beyond the borderline of validity ... one of Miss Streisand's major triumphs is her fresh approach to that old warhorse 'It Had to Be You': by taking it seriously, she has found a meaningfulness that seems to have escaped everyone who has been giving it the traditional vo-do-deo-do treatment all these years."

JOHN S. WILSON,
High Fidelity

"One track on the album suggests the singer Miss Streisand might become if she would only jettison all the clap-trap that now clutters her singing. This is 'Draw Me a Circle,' a superb piece of fresh material. She gets directly into its mood and projects it simply. Her singing, nearly free of vibrato, evokes a strange, abstracted mood that is exquisitely apropos. One feels for an instant that Miss Streisand could be as great as the press agents say she is."

GENE LEES,
Hi Fi/Stereo Review

FUNNY GIRL
(Capital Records Original Cast Recording, 1964)

PRODUCED FOR THE STAGE BY RAY STARK.
DIRECTED BY GARSON KANIN.
MUSIC BY JULE STYNE.
LYRICS BY BOB MERRILL.
MUSICAL DIRECTION BY MILTON ROSENSTOCK.
ORCHESTRATION BY RALPH BURNS.
VOCAL ARRANGEMENTS BY BUSTER DAVIS.
DANCE ORCHESTRATIONS BY LUTHER HENDERSON.
ALBUM PRODUCED BY DICK JONES.
CONDUCTED BY MILTON ROSENSTOCK.
PHOTOS BY HENRY GROSSMAN.
NOTES BY STANLEY GREEN.

SIDE 1

Overture
If a Girl Isn't Pretty
(*Stapleton, Medford, Meehan*)
I'm the Greatest Star
(*Streisand*)
Cornet Man
(*Streisand*)
Who Taught Her Everything?
(*Meehan, Medford*)
His Love Makes Me Beautiful
(*Streisand, Ensemble*)
I Want to Be Seen With You Tonight
(*Chaplin, Streisand*)
Henry Street
(*Ensemble*)
People
(*Streisand*)

SIDE 2

You Are Woman
(*Chaplin, Streisand*)
Don't Rain on My Parade
(*Streisand*)
Sadie, Sadie
(*Streisand, Ensemble*)
Find Yourself a Man
(*Medford, Meehan, Stapleton*)
Rat-tat-tat-tat
(*Meehan, Streisand, Ensemble*)
Who Are You Now?
(*Streisand*)
The Music That Makes Me Dance
(*Streisand*)
Don't Rain on My Parade—Reprise
(*Streisand*)

(Jule) Styne and Bob Merrill have written an impos-
et of songs for Miss Streisand, ranging from low
dy to big, wide-open emotionalism—on disc, the
is, in effect, a Streisand virtuoso performance.

She meets every challenge. She produces a tour-de-
of singing styles and devices on 'I'm the Greatest
She catches and projects a lusty music hall attack on
et Man.' . . . She also exhibits the strong, wide-rang-
inging style that has made her previous recordings so
tive. 'Don't Rain on My Parade' brings out the
ncy in her voice . . . the wonder is that she manages to
so many different vocal facets and, at the same time,
stain a strong sense of involvement in everything she
"

JOHN S. WILSON,
High Fidelity

PLE
lumbia, 1964)

DUCED BY ROBERT MERSEY.
RANGED AND CONDUCTED BY PETER MATZ
D RAY ELLIS.
COMPANIMENT BY PETER DANIELS.
ER PHOTO BY DON BRONSTEIN.
K COVER PHOTOS BY HANK PARKER.

E 1

sent-Minded Me
en in Rome (I Do as the Romans Do)

Fine and Dandy
Supper Time
Will He Like Me?
How Does the Wine Taste?

SIDE 2

I'm All Smiles
Autumn
My Lord and Master
Love Is a Bore
Don't Like Goodbyes
People

REVIEWS

"This is Barbra Streisand's fourth solo album. The
fact is worth mentioning because a singer who makes her
initial impact by being deliberately different . . . inevitably
loses much of her impact simply through the process of
repetition. Then what? Miss Streisand has weathered the
transition by her ability to invest practically anything with
a strong, personal and valid quality. Most of this collection
is devoted to good songs that are seldom heard or just
coming into their own. . . . By and large, Miss Streisand
has a kind of authority rare in a popular singer, including
the ability to improve on a good performance (a new and
excellent version of her *Funny Girl* hit, 'People,' is
included here). She has no need of gimmicks, oddities or
other crutches. That same skill that made her early inno-
vations seem valid makes these straight presentations just
as brilliant."

JOHN S. WILSON,
High Fidelity

"This is the least ugly recording Barbra Streisand has
yet made. . . . Of course, some of her worst qualities are
still in evidence—the adenoidal high notes, the deep breath-
ing into the mike, and the grab-bag of cheap histrionic
tricks. But I'm beginning to wonder whether this is the
fault of Miss Streisand or her recording director . . . the
sound quality is nutty. . . . Some day, if the business boys
don't goof her up, Miss Streisand may become a great
artist. But the day is not yet."

GENE LEES,
Hi Fi/Stereo Review

MY NAME IS BARBRA
(Columbia, 1965)

PRODUCED FOR TELEVISION BY RICHARD LEWINE.
ALBUM PRODUCED BY ROBERT MERSEY.
ARRANGED AND CONDUCTED BY PETER MATZ.
COVER PHOTOGRAPH BY SHELDON STREISAND.
BACK COVER PHOTOGRAPHS BY PETER OLIVER.

SIDE 1

My Name is Barbra
A Kid Again/I'm Five
Jenny Rebecca
My Pa
Sweet Zoo
Where Is the Wonder?

SIDE 2

I Can See It
Someone to Watch Over Me
I've Got No Strings
If You Were the Only Boy in the World
Why Did I Choose You?
My Man

REVIEWS

"The more I hear Miss Streisand, the more incredible it seems that this remarkable singing talent apparently just burst, full-blown, from a relatively untrained girl whose goal, insofar as she had one, was to be an actress. Every new recording reveals her as a singer who continues to grow in vocal control and in her ability to project a variety of moods. . . . One side is devoted to songs of childhood, the other to more mature thoughts of love. On the first side the penetrating purity of her voice enables her to sound childlike without being childish . . . she has more opportunity to use the fuller resources of her voice on the second side, particularly when she lofts 'I Can See It' or builds to a strong climax on 'My Man.'"

JOHN S. WILSON
High Fidelity

"The lady is wonderful. Her songs are pure magic and she can handle effortlessly the total range of emotion. She has a splendid chance to show her versatility in this unusual collection of tunes which runs the gamut from pixie-like youth to the rich ardor of true love. . . . I've only one piece of advice concerning this . . . buy it!"

FRED REYNOLDS
American Record Guide

MY NAME IS BARBRA, TWO
(Columbia, 1965)

PRODUCED BY ROBERT MERSEY.
ARRANGED AND CONDUCTED BY PETER MATZ AND DON COSTA.
COVER PHOTO BY ROGER PRIGENT.

SIDE 1

He Touched Me
The Shadow of Your Smile
Quiet Night
I Got Plenty of Nothin'
How Much of the Dream Comes True
Second Hand Rose

SIDE 2

The Kind of Man a Woman Needs
All That I Want

Where's That Rainbow
No More Songs for Me
Medley: Second Hand Rose/Give Me the
 Simple Life/I Got Plenty of Nothin'/
 Brother Can You Spare a Dime?/Nobody
 Knows You When You're Down and Out/
 Second Hand Rose/The Best Things in
 Life Are Free

REVIEWS

"This is a punny title sequel to the first LP based on
Barbra Streisand's CBS-TV special of several months ago.
This contains a medley of seven songs from that show, in
addition to a group of newly recorded ballads. Once again,
Miss Streisand gives a bowl-em-over vocal workout, hit-
ing with all types of material."

Variety

"If sequels fail, Barbra the bold dwells in bliss igno-
rant. *My Name is Barbra, Two* adds still more to an auda-
ciously incomparable body of work. Torch, soul, self-anal-
ysis—and still room for the hilariously sardonic 'Second
Hand Rose.' No hand-me-downs here!"

GREER JOHNSON,
Cue

COLOR ME BARBRA
(Columbia, 1966)

PRODUCED FOR TELEVISION BY JOE LAYTON AND
DWIGHT HEMION.
ALBUM COVER DRAWING BY ELINOR BUNIN.

SIDE 1

Yesterdays
One Kiss
The Minute Waltz

Gotta Move
Non C'est Rien
Where or When

SIDE 2

Medley: Animal Crackers in My Soup/Funny
 Face/That Face/They Didn't Believe Me/Were
 Thine That Special Face/I've Grown Accus-
 tomed to Her Face/Let's Face the Music
 and Dance/Sam, You Made the Pants Too
 Long/What's New Pussycat?/Small World/I
 Love You/I Stayed Too Long at the Fair/Look
 at That Face.
C'est Si Bon
Where Am I Going?
Starting Here, Starting Now

REVIEWS

"This issue, taken from her latest TV showcase,
leaped to first place on the music business' best-selling disc
charts on the heels of the show's generally excellent
reviews. But it does not follow that good commercial
sense is good artistic sense. In this case, the record buyer is
getting something less than he might have if Miss Streis-
and had planned a program for recording purposes alone.
On the TV screen, Miss Streisand's songs were an accompaniment—sometimes a background to—a swiftly moving
production with unusually strong visual values. There are
things on the disc that Miss Streisand probably would not
have done if she had been thinking in recording terms: a
long medley of vagrant lines from nine songs, mostly
involving the word 'face'—good songs, well sung, effective
in the TV context but meaningless on the disc; ... (and)
the orchestrated overbalance which Miss Streisand has to
fight on 'Yesterdays' and 'Where Am I Going?' ...

"This still leaves quite a bit that is effective in both
media. . . ."

JOHN S. WILSON,
High Fidelity

"*Color Me Barbra* is the most recent souvenir of Miss
Streisand's conquest of the world ... the entire album is
filled with memorable flashes of incredible beauty."

EDWARD JABLONSKI,
American Record Guide

JE M'APPELLE BARBRA
(Columbia, 1966)

PRODUCED BY ETTORE STRATTA.
ARRANGED AND CONDUCTED BY MICHEL LEGRAND.
COVER PHOTO BY RICHARD AVEDON.
LINER NOTES BY MAURICE CHEVALIER AND
NAT SHAPIRO.
BACK COVER PHOTO BY BRYAN DALY.
"WHAT NOW, MY LOVE?"
ARRANGED AND CONDUCTED BY RAY ELLIS.

SIDE 1

Free Again
Autumn Leaves
What Now, My Love?
Ma Premiere Chanson
Clopin Clopant
Le Mur

SIDE 2

I Wish You Love
Speak to Me of Love
Love and Learn
Once Upon a Summertime
Martina
I've Been Here

REVIEWS

"It's true that Miss Streisand's success has set off an unpleasant melee of sobbing, shrieking girl singers. At the same time, she is associated with fresh material and superb orchestrations, and even the worst of her imitators put out albums with lush arrangements. . . . Miss Streisand sings both English and French. Her French is excellent. Among the best tracks are 'Free Again,' 'Martina,' 'Autumn Leaves' and 'Clopin, Clopant.' Unfortunately, Miss Strei-

sand insists on screaming her way out of 'I Wish You Love' and 'What Now, My Love?', lowering an otherwise tasteful level. In her soft moments, however, she never sounded better. Nat Shapiro's liner notes give a complete picture of the material included. This was a powerful album idea and over-all, it's well executed. It's the best of the recent Streisand albums."

GENE LEES,
High Fidelity

" . . . A standout program of French ballads. Miss Streisand's knack for spine-tingling dramatizations is brilliantly demonstrated on songs like 'Autumn Leaves,' 'What Now, My Love?', 'I've Been Here,' 'I Wish You Love' . . . also striking is 'Ma Premiere Chanson,' written by Miss Streisand . . ."

Variety

SIMPLY STREISAND
(Columbia, 1967)

PRODUCED BY JACK GOLD AND HOWARD A.
ROBERTS.
ARRANGED BY RAY ELLIS.
CONDUCTED BY DAVID SHIRE.
ENGINEERED BY FRANK LAICO AND
RAY GERHARDT.
COVER PHOTO BY JAMES MOORE.
NOTES BY RICHARD ROGERS.

SIDE 1

My Funny Valentine
The Nearness of You
When Sunny Gets Blue
Make the Man Love Me
Lover Man

SIDE 2

More Than You Know
I'll Know
All the Things You Are
The Boy Next Door
Stout-Hearted Men

REVIEWS

"Streisand fans are in a quandary again. Recently she put out a single record that didn't work—'Stout Hearted Men'—attempting to plumb new depths from a song that never meant to be deep. . . . Now she has released an album of strictly standards—no surprises, no daring new treatments (except for 'Stout Hearted Men'). Even before this disc's release, rumor in the business said that it was bad.

"It's not bad at all. The fact is that Miss Streisand has thrown people off the track by singing straight. The characteristic sobs, gasps and so on are all but absent, and what embellishments she does inject are tentative, searching. The truth is that this is a transition album. Miss Streisand knows where's she's been, but she's undecided about where she's going. It's a valid search; it happens to all talents who are in this game for the long, not the short, run. Miss Streisand has already proved that she's a good actress. The interesting thing about this album is its implication that she's almost ready to become a full-fledged singer as well."

MORGAN AMES,
High Fidelity

". . . In our midst a young girl named Barbra Streisand is working as a functioning creative artist in media which seldom demand so high a level of self-expression to achieve success. . . . This album will eventually form part of the Streisand legacy. I think it will retain its relevance, as do so many of the recordings of Piaf, Brice, Morgan, Sinatra, Etting and Lee, because, you see, it is *about* something: it is about what a great performer feels about a given song."

PETER REILLY,
Hi Fi/Stereo Review

A CHRISTMAS ALBUM
(Columbia, 1967)

PRODUCED BY JACK GOLD.
ARRANGED AND CONDUCTED BY MARTY PAICH.
SIDE 2 NUMBERS PRODUCED BY ETTORE STRATTA AND ARRANGED AND CONDUCTED BY RAY ELLIS.
ENGINEERED BY RAFAEL O. VALENTIN AND JACK LATTIG.
COVER PHOTO BY HORN/GRINER.

SIDE 1

Jingle Bells?
Have Yourself a Merry Little Christmas
The Christmas Song (Chestnuts Roasting on an Open Fire)
White Christmas
My Favorite Things
The Best Gift

SIDE 2

Sleep in Heavenly Peace (Silent Night)
Gounod's Ave Maria
O Little Town of Bethlehem
I Wonder as I Wander
The Lord's Prayer.

REVIEWS

"Barbra Streisand. One loves her, sometimes wants to spank her, but not for her *A Christmas Album*. She seldom has sung so well and honestly as she does with a Side One of decorative trivia and a stunning Side Two elevated by John Joseph Niles's 'I Wonder as I Wander.' . . ."

GREER JOHNSON,
Cue

"Barbra shines in this LP, which should be a Christmas best seller in short order. Her treatments of 'The Christmas Song,' 'The Lord's Prayer' and 'Ave Maria' are made stirring by her rich tone. Also included is 'Sleep in Heavenly Peace,' from her best-selling Yule single."

Billboard

A HAPPENING IN CENTRAL PARK
(Columbia, 1968)

PRODUCED FOR TELEVISION BY ROBERT SCHEERER.
MUSICAL DIRECTION BY MORT LINDSEY.
ALBUM PRODUCED BY JACK GOLD.
SOUND SUPERVISION BY WARREN VINCENT.
ENGINEERED BY EDWARD T. GRAHAM, STAN
WEISS, PHIL MACY AND ARTHUR KENNEDY.
COVER PHOTO BY THE NEW YORK TIMES.

SIDE 1

I Can See It
New Love Is Like a Newborn Child
Folk Monologue/Value
Cry Me a River
People

SIDE 2

He Touched Me
Marty the Martian
Natural Sounds
Second Hand Rose
Sleep in Heavenly Peace
Happy Days Are Here Again

REVIEWS

"Barbra's *A Happening in Central Park* descends, as
readily as she does, into unintentionally self-demeaning
gags and defensive girlish postures she has, with her talented will, atomized. Thanks to a beer company, thou-
sands of persons heard her free in the park and she—who
knows?—may have been overwhelmed by the turnout.
The nasal clowning is miles removed from the beautiful
're-creation' of Fanny Brice on *Funny Girl*."

GREER JOHNSON,
Cue

"This stanza, recorded at a performance at a Central
Park concert last summer, shapes up as another sock b.o.
album by Barbra Streisand. She sings and talks, but above
all, she sings with her customary brilliance on songs like
'Second Hand Rose,' 'Cry Me a River,' 'Silent Night' and
'People.' She also displays her comedic talents in the 'Folk
Monologue—Value.'"

Variety

FUNNY GIRL
(Columbia, 1968)

ORIGINAL SOUNDTRACK RECORDING OF A COLUMBIA
PICTURE.
PRODUCED BY WILLIAM WYLER AND RAY STARK.
MUSIC BY JULE STYNE, LYRICS BY BOB MERRILL.
MUSICAL NUMBERS DIRECTED BY HERBERT ROSS.
MUSICAL SUPERVISION BY WALTER SCHARF.
ALBUM ENGINEERED BY STAN WEISS.
NOTES BY JACK BRODSKY.

SIDE 1

Overture
I'm the Greatest Star
(*Streisand*)
If a Girl Isn't Pretty
(*Medford, Questel*)
Roller Skate Rag
(*Ensemble*)
I'd Rather Be Blue Over You (Than
Happy With Somebody Else)
(*Streisand*)
His Love Makes Me Beautiful
(*Streisand, Ensemble*)

SIDE 2

People
(*Streisand*)
You Are Woman, I Am Man
(*Sharif, Streisand*)

on't Rain on My Parade
treisand)

die, Sadie
treisand, Sharif)

he Swan
treisand)

nny Girl
treisand)

y Man
treisand)

nale

REVIEWS

"No doubt some purists will think the Broadway
bum version of *Funny Girl* was 'truer' than this one. But
is one is better. Even Miss Streisand is better in this ver-
on. I am scarcely one of her admirers, but I like her here.
omebody has toned down her stridency, honed her taste.
nd, of course, her comic flair—which comes across in
he album quite well—is one of her biggest talents."

GENE LEES,
High Fidelity

"The *Funny Girl* soundtrack is good. It is very good.
t contains the new numbers, which are also good; and it
resents Barbra Streisand under the rigid control of a
najor production, which is good for Miss Streisand. Here
ve confront what soundtrack albums should be about: the
erformer, the story, the material, and the essence. . . ."

GREER JOHNSON,
Cue

WHAT ABOUT TODAY?
(Columbia, 1969)

PRODUCED BY WALLY GOLD.

ARRANGED AND CONDUCTED BY PETER MATZ,
WITH DON COSTA AND MICHEL LEGRAND.

PHOTOS BY RICHARD AVEDON.

ENGINEERED BY DON MEEHAN.

NOTES BY BARBRA STREISAND.

SIDE 1

What About Today?
Ask Yourself Why
Honey Pie
Punky's Dilemma
Until It's Time For You to Go
That's a Fine Kind of Freedom

SIDE 2

Little Tin Soldier
With a Little Help From My Friends
Alfie
The Morning After
Goodnight

REVIEWS

". . . *What About Today* was the star's pops disc of
the year. Hardly a loss, it nevertheless demonstrates that a
powerhouse singer like Barbra Streisand thrives best with
powerhouse programs. She tends to overwhelm flaccid and
semi-professional ephemerae."

GREER JOHNSON,
Cue

"Barbra Streisand, whose sound is always distinctive,
has moved into the contemporary bag with a vengeance,
on her new set. . . . The songstress' vocalizing is dramatic
and sizzling, and, with this album, she's in a brand new
bag, the color of which looks gold."

Cash Box

HELLO, DOLLY!
(20th Century-Fox Records, 1969)

ORIGINAL SOUNDTRACK RECORDING OF A 20TH
CENTURY—FOX PICTURE.
PRODUCED BY ERNEST LEHMAN AND DIRECTED
BY GENE KELLY.
MUSIC AND LYRICS BY JERRY HERMAN.
MUSICAL NUMBERS STAGED BY MICHAEL KIDD.
CONDUCTED BY LENNIE HAYTON
AND LIONEL NEWMAN.
ALBUM ENGINEERED BY MURRAY SPIVAK.

SIDE 1

Just Leave Everything to Me
(*Streisand*)
It Takes a Woman
(*Matthau*)
It Takes a Woman—Reprise
(*Streisand*)
Put on Your Sunday Clothes
(*Streisand, Ensemble*)
Ribbons Down My Back
(*McAndrew*)
Dancing
(*Streisand, Crawford, Lockin, Ensemble*)
Before the Parade Passes By
(*Streisand*)

SIDE 2

Elegance
(*Crawford, Lockin, Peaker, McAndrew*)
Love Is Only Love
(*Streisand*)
Hello, Dolly!
(*Streisand, Armstrong, Ensemble*)
It Only Takes a Moment
(*Crawford, McAndrew*)
So Long Dearie
(*Streisand*)
Finale
(*Ensemble*)

REVIEWS

"Barbra Streisand's middle name is 'special,' as the
soundtrack album of the film version of *Hello, Dolly!*
makes vibrantly clear. Properly, this is *her* glorified
parade, and nothing passes her by. Of the major stars who
have recorded Dolly, Carol Channing is more fanciful and
Pearl Bailey is earthier and wiser; irrepressible Barbra goes
her own way—youthful, direct, romantic and humorous at
times with a Mae Westian accent. . . . It's Miss Streisand's
picnic throughout, and she never lets it elude her control."

GREER JOHNSON,
Cue

"The parlay of this click Broadway musical score b
Jerry Herman and Barbra Streisand in the title role ad
up to a powerhouse soundtrack album. . . . And as
clincher, Louis Armstrong, who had the smash single h
on the show's title song, also gets a solid crack at the sor
again in an elaborate production number in which b
duets with Miss Streisand. She completely dominates th
album. . . ."

Variet

BARBRA STREISAND'S GREATEST HITS
(Columbia, 1970)

PRODUCED BY ROBERT MERSEY, ETTORE STRATTA,
JACK GOLD, WARREN VINCENT.
ARRANGED AND CONDUCTED BY PETER MATZ,
MICHEL LEGRAND, DON COSTA.
SOUND SUPERVISED BY WARREN VINCENT.
ENGINEERED BY FRANK LAICO AND STAN WEISS.
COVER PHOTOGRAPH BY LAWRENCE SCHILLER.

SIDE 1

People
Second Hand Rose
Why Did I Choose You?
He Touched Me
Free Again
Don't Rain on My Parade

SIDE 2

My Coloring Book
Sam, You Made the Pants Too Long
My Man
Gotta Move
Happy Days Are Here Again

"At long last . . . a collection of Barbra Streisand's
most outstanding single performances, and they're all
here! From her sensitive 'People' and 'Happy Days Are
Here Again' to the bouncy and infectious 'Second Hand
Rose' and 'Sam, You Made the Pants Too Long,' this
package is destined to prove an immediate chart winner,
and remain a top seller for some time to come."

Billboard

"For a true Streisand fan, picking up on this item will
be like picking up a piece of heaven on earth. . . . A well-
done editing job from the tome of material on her twelve
previous albums."

Cash Box

ON A CLEAR DAY YOU CAN SEE FOREVER
(Columbia, 1970)

ORIGINAL SOUNDTRACK RECORDING OF A
PARAMOUNT PICTURE.
PRODUCED BY HOWARD W. KOCH AND ALAN JAY
LERNER, AND DIRECTED BY VINCENTE
MINNELLI.
MUSIC BY BURTON LANE, LYRICS BY
ALAN JAY LERNER.
ARRANGED AND CONDUCTED BY NELSON RIDDLE.
ALBUM ENGINEERED BY DON MEEHAN.
NOTES BY CHARLES BURR.

SIDE 1

Hurry! It's Lovely Up Here!
(Streisand)

Main Title—On a Clear Day
(Chorus)

Love With All the Trimmings
(Streisand)

Melinda
(Montand)

Go to Sleep
(Streisand)

SIDE 2

He Isn't You
(Streisand)

What Did I Have That I Don't Have?
(Streisand)

Come Back to Me
(Montand)

On a Clear Day
(Montand)

On a Clear Day
(Streisand)

REVIEWS

"Surprise . . . here is that rarity, a show-based album
actually geared for living-room listening. True, Barbra
Streisand goes all-out Broadway on the title tune and
other spots as required, but over-all, her singing shows
unexpected and pleasing restraint. Yves Montand's tracks
. . . are at best charming—and at least charming. Like the
film, the album is a rather appealing compromise of diverse
aspects of entertainment and I recommend it."

MORGAN AMES,
High Fidelity

"This package of the film soundtrack has a surefire
commercial angle in the starring performance of Barbra
Streisand. Miss Streisand is spotlighted on the title song,
which she delivers with even more of her distinctive
inflections than usual. She also has sock impact on 'Love
With All the Trimmings,' 'Go to Sleep,' 'He Isn't You'
and 'What Did I Have That I Don't Have?'"

Variety

THE OWL AND THE PUSSYCAT
(Columbia, 1971)

ORIGINAL SOUNDTRACK RECORDING OF A COLUMBIA
PICTURE.
PRODUCED BY RAY STARK AND DIRECTED BY
HERBERT ROSS.
COMEDY HIGHLIGHTS FROM THE SCREENPLAY
BY BUCK HENRY.
MUSIC COMPOSED AND ARRANGED BY
RICHARD HALLIGAN.
PERFORMED BY BLOOD, SWEAT AND TEARS.
ALBUM PRODUCED BY THOMAS Z. SHEPARD.
ENGINEERED BY ARTHUR KENDY.
NOTES BY STEVE SCHIFFMAN.
BACK COVER ILLUSTRATION BY AL HIRSCHFELD.

SIDE 1

The Confrontation
The Warmup
The Seduction

SIDE 2

The Morning After
The Reunion

REVIEW

"The movie—groovy, bantamweight, and thoroughly
inconsequential—has a generosity of hilarious moments
with first-rate comedienne Streisand and master-of-long-
suffering George Segal performing deliciously together.
But its very plot development is founded on a succession
of zany 'sight tricks': Streisand's unbelievable nightwear,
Segal's TV programming through a tropical fishtank,
Segal and Streisand's boudoir acrobatics and bathe-in, to

mention but a few. The banter heard on this reco
therefore, is apt to leave one in a state of bafflement rat
than bemusement. What *does* work well here is the sou
soundtrack of Blood, Sweat and Tears, which is gen
ously interlarded with the slivers of dialogue."

STEPHEN POTTE
American Record Gu

STONEY END
(Columbia, 1971)

PRODUCED BY RICHARD PERRY.
MUSIC ARRANGED BY GENE PAGE, PERRY BOTK
JR., CLAUS OGERMAN.
ALBUM ENGINEERED BY GLEN KOLOTKIN,
RAFAEL O. VALENTIN, SY MITCHELL, PETE WEI
BOB BREAULT.
DESIGN AND PHOTOGRAPHY BY TOM WILKES
AND BARRY FEINSTEIN FOR
CAMOUFLAGE PRODUCTIONS.

SIDE 1

I Don't Know Where I Stand
Hands Off the Man (Flim Flam Man)
If You Could Read My Mind
Just a Little Lovin'
Let Me Go
Stoney End

SIDE 2

No Easy Way Down
Time and Love
Maybe
Free the People
I'll Be Home

REVIEWS

"Having scored heavily with Laura Nyro's 'Ston
End,' Miss Streisand logically follows with an LP of co
temporary material and further demonstrates that she is
singer of any day ... Randy Newman's 'I'll Be Home' a
Nilsson's 'Maybe' are beautifully sung."

Billboa

"*Stoney End* is a lovely, listenable, often exciti
album that does absolutely everybody justice ... t
gentle innocence Barbra brings to (for example) Jo
Mitchell's 'I Don't Know Where I Stand' raises that lad
song to a polished level she has never been able to rea
with it herself. ... Barbra invests so much energy, d
covers so many subtle and fragrant details, and displays
many lyrical attitudes in this program that almost eve
song sounds better than it ever has before."

REX REE
Stereo Revie

BARBRA JOAN STREISAND
(Columbia, 1971)

PRODUCED BY RICHARD PERRY.
ENGINEERED BY SY MITCHELL, BILL SCHNEE,
GEORGE BEAUREGARD, WILLIE GREER, JOHN FIORE,
JACK ANDREWS.
DESIGNED BY VIRGINIA TEAM.
PHOTOGRAPHY BY ED THRASHER.

SIDE 1

Beautiful
Love
Where You Lead
I Never Meant to Hurt You
One Less Bell to Answer/A House Is
Not a Home

SIDE 2

Space Captain
Since I Fell For You
Mother
The Summer Knows
I Mean to Shine
You've Got a Friend

REVIEWS

"Like all of Barbra Streisand's albums, *Barbra Joan Streisand* is an expertly produced commercial product designed for the widest possible audience. . . . It comes in a studiedly casual, though glamorous, visual package . . . the whole turns out to be an uneasy mix. . . . An unqualified bummer is Barbra's rendition of John Lennon's 'Mother,' in which she 'belts out' the primal scream. A mechanized shriek that has all the humanity of a police siren, it makes an embarrassing mockery of a great song.

"The high point of the album, the Bacharach-David medley, is pure vintage Streisand. A duet with herself, she croons it like it is for all the male models and Marjorie Morningstars of this world with kleig lights in their eyes. Everything works together to achieve the ultimate in pop professionalism. More than Dionne Warwick even, Barbra Streisand would seem to be the singer best suited to record the complete Burt Bacharach-Hal David songbook. It would be the crowning achievement of her career. As for the Carole King or John Lennon songbooks, god forbid."

STEPHEN HOLDEN,
Rolling Stone

"To say that this is a 'new Streisand' implies that she has shed an old self. Yes and no—mostly no. What this album displays is an alive and growing Streisand. Because of that, she will appeal most to the young and to those with open and still-growing minds. Naturally that means you."

MORGAN AMES,
High Fidelity

LIVE CONCERT AT THE FORUM
(Columbia, 1972)

PRODUCED BY RICHARD PERRY.
CONDUCTED BY DAVID SHIRE.
VOCAL DIRECTION BY EDDIE KENDRIX.
ENGINEERED BY BILL SCHNEE.
BACKGROUND BY THE EDDIE KENDRIX SINGERS.
COVER ILLUSTRATION BY ROBERT REDDING.
INSIDE PHOTOS BY STEVE SCHAPIRO.
NOTES BY MORT GOODE.

SIDE 1

Sing/Make Your Own Kind of Music
Starting Here, Starting Now
Don't Rain on My Parade
Monologue
On a Clear Day (You Can See Forever)
Sweet Inspiration/Where You Lead

SIDE 2

Didn't We
My Man
Stoney End
Sing/Happy Days Are Here Again
People

REVIEWS

". . . A winner all the way. Barbra Streisand is at the top of her dramatic form on an excellent choice of contemporary and standard ballads. Standouts are 'Sing/Make Your Own Kind of Music,' 'Starting Here, Starting Now,' 'On a Clear Day,' 'My Man,' 'People' and 'Sweet Inspiration/Where You Lead.' "

Variety

"So many of the pop singers of the day could learn something about the use of dynamics in singing from Miss Streisand who, in her latest offering, shows again her great control in this department. Although she includes some of her by now too familiar material . . . there are also Carole King's 'Where You Lead,' her rock hit 'Stoney End,' and 'Sing' from *Sesame Street*. This live concert may not be so well recorded as most of Barbra's studio albums but it benefits greatly from her superb showmanship and her empathetic rapport with an audience. A Streisand triumph."

Movie Digest

BARBRA STREISAND . . . AND OTHER MUSICAL INSTRUMENTS
(Columbia, 1973)

PRODUCED FOR TELEVISION BY GARY SMITH AND DWIGHT HEMION.
ALBUM PRODUCED BY MARTIN ERLICHMAN.
MUSICAL MATERIALS WRITTEN AND ARRANGED BY KEN AND MITZIE WELCH.
MUSICAL DIRECTION BY JACK PARNELL.
SOUND DIRECTOR: BILL NUTTALL.
SOUND MIXER: BILL SCHNEE.
INSIDE PHOTOGRAPH BY BARON WOLMAN.
NOTES BY MORT GOODE.

SIDE 1

Piano Practicing
I Got Rhythm
Johnny One Note/One Note Samba
Glad to Be Unhappy
People
Second Hand Rose
Don't Rain on My Parade

SIDE 2

Don't Ever Leave Me
Monologue/By Myself
Come Back to Me
I Never Has Seen Snow
Auf dem Wasser zu Singen
The World Is a Concerto/Make Your Own Kind of Music
The Sweetest Sounds

REVIEW

"Smothered in 'production values' and self-importance, our Barbra is a mess on her latest Columbia LP, *Barbra Streisand and Other Musical Instruments*, actually the soundtrack of her recent TV special. Accompanied by bells, gongs, finger cymbals (she fingers them herself) and all sorts of exotic instruments from far-off lands, including some electrical appliances from this land and an orchestra of symphonic proportions, she is unable to sing effectively . . . The appliances? Well, there's a number here entitled 'The World is a Concerto,' an even worse piece of material than Tony Martin's numbing 'Tenement Symphony' of dreaded memory, and it's based on the principle that all the everyday gadgets we deal with create a music of their own (though how 'Concerto' gets into this, I don't know).

"Barbra sort of drifts through all this and several other fine songs . . . as though she isn't quite sure where she is but feels friendly and even eager to join in with all the nutty stuff going on around her. The result is an unbelievably mannered and silly concert which we'll just put down as one of those awful mistakes stars make, or are thrust into, at least once in their careers."

DOUGLAS WATT
New York Sunday News

88

BARBRA'S SINGLES

When the Sun Comes Out
Happy Days Are Here Again

My Coloring Book
Lover Come Back to Me

*Happy Days Are Here Again
My Coloring Book

People
I Am Woman

Absent-Minded Me
Funny Girl

Why Did I Choose You?
My Love

*People
Second Hand Rose

My Man
Where Is the Wonder?

He Touched Me
I Like Him

Second Hand Rose
The Kind of Man a Woman Needs

Where Am I Going?
You Wanna Bet?

The Minute Waltz
Sam, You Made the Pants Too Long

Non, C'est Rien
Le Mur

Free Again
I've Been Here

Sleep in Heavenly Peace
Gounod's Ave Maria

Stout-Hearted Men
Look

Lover Man
My Funny Valentine

Jingle Bells?
White Christmas

Have Yourself a Merry Little Christmas
The Best Gift

My Favorite Things
The Christmas Song

The Lord's Prayer
I Wonder as I Wander

Our Corner of the Night
He Could Show Me

The Morning After
Where Is the Wonder?

*Funny Girl
I'd Rather Be Blue

*My Man
Don't Rain on My Parade

Frank Mills
Punky's Dilemma

Little Tin Soldier
Honey Pie

What Are You Doing
the Rest of Your Life?
What About Today?

Before the Parade Passes By
Love Is Only Love

The Best Thing
You've Ever Done
Summer Me, Winter Me

Stoney End
I'll Be Home

Time and Love
No Easy Way Down

Flim Flam Man
Maybe

Where You Lead
Since I Fell For You

*The Best Thing You've Ever Done
What Are You Doing the Rest of Your Life?

*Stoney End
Time and Love

Mother
The Summer Knows

Space Captain
One Less Bell to Answer/A House Is Not a Home

Sweet Inspiration/Where You Lead
Didn't We

Sing/Make Your Own Kind of Music
Starting Here, Starting Now

Didn't We
On a Clear Day

If I Close My Eyes
If I Close My Eyes—Instrumental

The Way We Were
What Are You Doing the Rest of Your Life?

NOTES

Songs by Barbra have also appeared
on the following non-Streisand albums:

The Best of '66
The Shadow of Your Smile

Harold Sings Arlen (With Friend)
Ding Dong the Witch Is Dead
House of Flowers

*Our Best to You—Today's Great
Hits ... Today's Great Stars*
I Wish You Love

Songs for a Summer Night
My Coloring Book

*The Greatest Hits of the '60s—
40 Great Stars—40 Great Hits*
Alfie

Season's Best
The Christmas Song

Show Time/Best of Broadway
Miss Marmelstein

The American Musical Theatre
Nobody Makes a Pass at Me

*HALL OF FAME SINGLES—STILL AVAILABLE

Barbra appearing on The Joe Franklin Show early in 1963, with Rudy Vallee and Jack LaLanne. Franklin was one of Barbra's earliest advocates.

ter her great success on Broadway and records, evision was a frontier Barbra *had* to conquer. Many her critics had contended that the intimacy of the evision cameras would not be flattering to Barbra's usual looks and unique style. But Barbra proved the nics wrong with successful guest appearances and a umphant solo spectacular. Intimacy only enhanced r appeal, and the national audience was entranced. levision was Barbra's biggest stepping stone Hollywood stardom. Had she failed on TV, e more than likely would not have been given the portunity to star in movies.

Barbra made her first television appearance on oril 5, 1961 on *The Jack Paar Show*, sharing the otlight with Phyllis Diller and guest host Orson an. Her sensational appearances at the Lion and Bon ir had brought her to the attention of several New ork-based shows, and she began appearing regularly Mike Wallace's *PM East* and *The David Susskind* ow. She quickly gained a reputation as "that nut m TV." She would wear some new thrift shop ery for each appearance—for one, an oversized, ppy hat, for another, an exotic fur stole, for still other, an 1890s dressing gown. Her views as well ent a long way toward making her one of late-night V's most colorful and controversial guests. On one Wallace's shows, she launched into a blistering ade against milk, on another she administered a ychological test to the other guests to determine if ey were schizophrenic. Once, she said to David sskind, "I scare you, don't I? I'm so far out I'm in."

In addition to all this deliberate nonconformism, course, Barbra also sang—in the same exciting style hich had enthralled her nightclub audiences. Very uch in demand, Barbra appeared no fewer than teen times on *PM East* during 1961.

Before long, Barbra made the ascent from local to tional TV. She did guest stints on the prime-time eeklies of Dinah Shore, Garry Moore, Bob Hope and I Sullivan, introducing people across the country to r unique style. On October 6, 1963, she appeared on e new *Judy Garland Show*, and her performance ade show business history.

Mel Tormé, in his book *The Other Side of the inbow*, tells us that Judy was apprehensive about orking with Streisand, who was being called the new nging sensation and, more importantly, was being mpared favorably to Garland. Judy called Tormé to r trailer on the set early one morning. Listening to rbra's recording of "Happy Days," Garland sug- sted she juxtapose "Get Happy" along with it and ondered, tentatively, if Streisand would approve. ormé quotes himself as saying, "She'd be out of her ind if she didn't."

Barbra did approve, and it turned out to be one of e high spots in a totally successful hour. Barbra was

With Bob Hope before filming her appearance on his special in 1963

The marquee at the CBS studios where My Name is Barbra was taped.

Streisand special—My Name is Barbra

introduced while Judy sang "Be My Guest." When Judy told her that she could do anything she wanted, Barbra replied "Can I replace you?" She then joined Judy in singing "Be My Guest" to welcome her co-stars, the Smothers Brothers.

Later, Barbra appeared on stage against a black background with one small spotlight trained on her face. She sang a moving "Bewitched, Bothered and Bewildered" with a voice of such pure and beautiful timbre that it left one in awe. Completing that mellow number, she then ripped into "Down With Love," in which she more than adequately lived up to her reputation as an "emotional singer." She performed the song as a three-act play, with grimaces, tosses of the head, clenched fists, coy and ironic smiles and bitter laughter. It was an enthralling, electric, exciting performance which left the audience gasping and reduced Judy Garland to the simple comment, "You're thrilling."

After the "Get Happy/Happy Days" duet, Ethel Merman joined Judy and Barbra during the "Tea Time" segment. Judy commented that Barbra and Merman were among the true "belters" of song and added, "There aren't many of us left." The three voices then got together for "There's No Business Like Show Business"–with Merman drowning out everybody, including the orchestra. Barbra tried to compete, but finally put her hand to her head in disbelief, happily conceding the "belter" crown to Merman. Streisand's appearance ended with a duet medley with Judy. Barbra sang "Hooray for Love," "By Myself," "How About You?," "Lover, Come Back to Me" and "It All Depends on You."

The result was, in Mel Tormé's words, "one of the few memorable shows in the series." Barbra was so good, in fact, that she won an Emmy nomination for the "Outstanding Performance in a Variety or Musical Program or Series." It was the first time in Emmy history that a guest appearance had won such a nomination.

Shortly after Barbra opened in *Funny Girl*, she signed an unprecedented $5 million contract with the Columbia Broadcasting System. The terms of the agreement called for Barbra to star in one television special a year during the next ten years. The extraordinary scope of the pact and the sum involved started show business tongues wagging. Many veterans felt that CBS was taking too big a risk on this girl. Although she had done very well in a few guest appearances, there was no guarantee that she could succeed as the star of her own specials. When her first production was announced as a one-woman spectacular, the skepticism was greatly strengthened.

On the evening of April 28, 1965, at 10:00 P.M., the American people were given their first long,

close-up look at Barbra Streisand. They were enthralled and delighted by what they saw. Rushing from set to set in a flowing gown singing "I'm Late," cavorting in a hugely oversized playground as a five-year-old, joking with the audience during a monolog about a weird lady called "Pearl from Istanbul," waltzing through Bergdorf Goodman's in assorted expensive outfits singing "Second Hand Rose" and finally performing in concert, Barbra proved herself to be one of the most exciting, talented performers in show business. *My Name Is Barbra* created a sensation across the country as reviewers outdid each other in praising the show and its star. One critic called it "The classic hour of entertainment in any field." New York's *Journal-American* ran a front-page photo the following day, with the caption "Magnificent Barbra."

At award time early the following year, *My Name Is Barbra* won five Emmys: "Outstanding Program"; "Outstanding Individual Achievement in Entertainment"–Barbra Streisand; "Best Concept, Choreography and Staging"–Joe Layton; "Best Art Design"–Tom John and Bill Harp; and "Best Musical Direction"–Peter Matz. Barbra, accepting her award, quipped, "When I used to watch these award shows as a kid, I'd look to see who was drunk. Now I'm up here myself."

More than most stars in the same situation, Barbra deserved credit for the phenomenal success of her first special. It was produced by Ellbar Productions, a company formed by the Goulds in order to assure complete creative control by Barbra over her specials.

Plans for the second Streisand spectacular were immediately drawn up. Deciding not to deviate from a successful formula, Barbra retained not only the same personnel, but the same basic format—three individual segments. For *Color Me Barbra*, these would have the star in the Philadelphia Museum of Art, at a zoo with various animals, and, as before, in an hour-ending concert.

Unanticipated production problems quickly arose once filming began. Only after the most delicate negotiations was permission to film in the Philadelphia Museum granted—for a strict limit of one weekend. The resultant hectic schedule forced Barbra and the crew to work for thirty-two straight hours to complete the filming by the deadline. The task wasn't helped by various mechanical failures, demands for interviews with Barbra, and everyone's frayed nerves. There were several near-misses as cables and other production equipment jeopardized priceless art treasures. Aside from a few frights for museum guards, however, no damage was done, and the filming was completed on schedule.

Part II saw Barbra singing a medley to various circus animals, and the filming became a comedy of

…hearsing a number for **The Belle of 14th Street** *with Jason Robards and the "Beef Trust Girls"*

…aotic terrors. The gymnast assigned to teach Barbra …mbling for a trampoline bit fell through the springs …d was injured. The penguins became sick under the …hts and had to be moved to a refrigerated area. A …ny fell, the elephants balked at performing and a …er escaped from his cage six times.

Finally, acceptable footage was obtained, and …rbra's concert was the only segment left to film. …o the CBS studios were brought 281 bleacher seats …d an audience comprised of members of Streisand … clubs—"We know *they'll* applaud," one of Bar- …a's press agents said.

The completed program, closely edited by Barbra …d the show's producers, was aired on CBS on March …, 1966. The critical reaction was that Barbra had …ualed, if not surpassed, her triumph in *My Name Is …rbra.* Wrote one reviewer: "In all truth, it takes a …eat personality, as well as a first-rate singer, to hold a …V show on the sheer strength of her own talents. …rbra Streisand did it magnificently in *Color Me …rbra.*"

Color Me Barbra, like its predecessor, garnered …ry high ratings and five Emmy nominations. The …ow lost out, however, in the major Emmy races to

Frank Sinatra's *A Man and His Music.*

Several months after giving birth to her son Jason in December 1966, Barbra began filming her third special. Originally entitled *The Barbra Streisand Show,* it was renamed *The Belle of 14th Street* and was, in many ways, a radical departure from Barbra's first two video efforts. Rather than three unrelated segments, *Belle* was to have a theme, the Golden Age of Vaudeville, and consist of a series of sketches related to that theme. It was also to be the first Streisand special to feature guest stars—Jason Robards, Lee Allen (who had played Eddie Ryan in the London *Funny Girl*) and vaudevillian John Bubbles.

Early in 1967, an advertisement was run in a half-dozen theatrical newspapers in Hollywood and New York:

WANTED. Weight Watchers Dropouts. Beefy Beauties needed for Barbra Streisand CBS-TV musical special. Must sing, dance, be under 45 (years) and over 45 (bust), and fracture the scales at 200 or more in soaking wet bikinis. Send snapshots with statistics.

The girls were needed for a planned re-creation of the vaudeville "Beef Trust" chorus, with Jason Robards as a song and dance man.

The Belle of 14th Street put Barbra into period costumes from the early 1900s, complete with feathery hats and boas, parasols and tassels. She imitated Irish colleens and German Fräuleins, played both Ariel and Miranda in a takeoff of Shakespeare's *The Tempest*. The songs were vintage evocations of the era: "My Melancholy Baby," "Some of These Days," "Put Your Arms Around Me Honey" and "Alice Blue Gown" were just a few.

When the special was aired on October 11, 1967, it met with near-unanimous panning from the critics. They assailed it for lack of substance, poor taste (the beef trust number) and boredom. Barbra's personal reviews were much better, especially in her solo concert at the show's end, and the reviewers suggested that Barbra would have been much better off alone. *The Belle of 14th Street* became Barbra's first failure of her first decade. Hardly anyone remembers the show today (there was never a soundtrack album released) and those who do suggest that the show was forgettable.

The single factor which most harmed *The Belle of 14th Street* is probably the fact that television audiences were not prepared for the format changes it presented. Along with the fact that most people would have preferred Barbra alone, it is easy to understand the critical response to the show. Standing alone, it is better than most people give it credit for.

On Friday, June 16, 1967, Barbra flew to New York City from the *Funny Girl* set in Hollywood. She was to appear the next night in concert at the 93-acre Sheep Meadow area of Central Park. At 6 A.M. Saturday morning, Streisand fans began arriving, and by concert time 135,000 people of all ages and walks of life had crowded into the park to hear Barbra sing, the largest audience ever assembled for a single performer anywhere in the world.

The concert was sponsored by Rheingold Beer, and was free to the public. The night became a triumph for Barbra, and one of the most exciting and memorable entertainment evenings in New York history. Barbra captured the minds and hearts of that vast audience, and some others, too—she stopped traffic blocks away as motorists slowed down to hear snatches of her songs.

The entire two-and-a-half-hour concert was filmed in color, to be televised as Barbra's fourth special. An hour show presenting the concert's best moments was aired on September 16, 1968, and won critical applause and high ratings. Barbra sang many of her popular favorites, held a sing-along with the audience on "Second Hand Rose," did a comic mono-

Barbra proudly displays the artwork sent to fans across the country following the airing of Me Barbra.

Part of the crowd of 135,000 which assembled Barbra's Central Park concert in June, 1967.

logue, sang a reprise of her *Another Evening with Harry Stoones* showstopper "Value," and introduced two beautiful new ballads, "New Love Is Like a Newborn Child" and "Natural Sounds." To the surprise and delight of that hot and muggy June audience, she sang a lovely "Silent Night," which was just as refreshing to the television audiences in September.

After her phenomenal success in the *Funny Girl* film, Barbra decided to devote herself to movies and her life-long dream of becoming a Hollywood star, and her television appearances have been few and far between. Her Oscar acceptance in 1969 was televised, as was her appearance to receive a special Tony Award later that year. Early in 1971, Streisand made her first guest appearance in many years on the Burt Bacharach Special. Dressed in a black pants suit, Barbra sang a duet with herself on a medley of "A House Is Not a Home" and "One Less Bell to Answer." She held a breathy exchange of admiration with Bacharach and did an impromptu duet with him of "Close to You." She capped her performance by singing a ballad written especially for her by Bacharach, "Be Aware." The show won an Emmy as Best Musical Program and its producers, accepting the award, thanked Barbra for her contributions to making the show a success.

Early in 1971, Barbra taped a two-hour interview with David Frost which was scheduled as a solo guest appearance on his late-night talk show. The program was never televised because of what was termed an "exclusivity" problem with CBS over Streisand's contract with them—they would not allow the program to be aired until the problem was worked out, and it never was. What was most likely a fascinating insight into Barbra Streisand will in all likelihood never be seen.

More than five years after *A Happening in Central Park*, on November 2, 1973, Barbra's fifth special was aired. In that five-year span, Barbra had become a movie superstar and an Oscar winner, and the show was eagerly awaited. Reunited for the effort were Dwight Hemion and Joe Layton, who had guided Barbra to success in her previous video efforts.

The theme of *Barbra Streisand . . . And Other Musical Instruments* was international music. Intended as a showcase for strange foreign instruments which would accompany Barbra's singing, the show was filmed during the summer of 1973.

And such a showcase it indeed was. The instruments—140 of them—were actually the stars of the hour, with Barbra reduced to a supporting role. The opening sequence, sixteen minutes long, used "I Got Rhythm" as a framework for an international tour. Turkish tumbaks and ouds were used with "People," Japanese kotos and o-daikos for "Glad to Be Unhappy," American Indian tom-toms and horn rattles for "Don't Rain on My Parade," East Indian crotales and ching ya-grins with "Johnny One Note/One Note Samba."

For each of the numbers, Barbra wore a costume

suitable to the country. All were designed from the same simple black dress, using dyes and ornamentation.

At the end of this segment, Barbra holds the final note of "I Got Rhythm" for an incredible twenty-two seconds—so long that during the initial filming of the number, she fainted upon completing it.

In the next segment, Barbra sings "Don't Ever Leave Me," and the musicians soon do, turning into electronic gadgets. Barbra sings "By Myself" and "Come Back to Me" in competition with a Moog synthesizer.

Ray Charles, Barbra's only guest, then joins her for "Look What They've Done to My Song, Ma" and "Cryin' Time." Charles' group, the Raeletts, then backed up Barbra for "Sweet Inspiration."

"Auf dem Wasser zu Singen," by Franz Schubert, had Barbra, complete with piano and hand fan, ask us to join her in singing it—following the bouncing ball over German lyrics. It was a charming ploy and great fun.

Barbra's next song—one of the few sung in its entirety and without gimmickry or ornamentation—was a beautiful ballad, "I Never Has Seen Snow," by Harold Arlen and Truman Capote. Emotionally sung, it highlighted Barbra's flair for dramatic lyrics.

The hour's final production number, "The World Is a Concerto," was written and conceived by Ken and Mitzie Welch. The "musical instruments" in this case were ordinary household appliances—orange juicers, steam kettles, sewing machines, a doorbell, electric shavers and hair dryers, among many others. The Welches' amusing lyrics were punctuated by the sounds generated by these items.

The hour ended with a backlighted, soft-focused Barbra singing "The Sweetest Sounds" while the credits rolled by.

Barbra Streisand . . . And Other Musical Instruments came across on the home screen as at best a mixed bag. The concept of using international instruments was indeed original and imaginative—and a refreshing change from the usual pallid "Special" fare. But the concept was ultimately better than its execution. In too many instances, the instruments merely distracted and annoyed the viewer. The strange sounds too often did little to complement the songs, and the resultant clash served only to negate the beauty of each.

Even more unsuccessful were the attempts to lump electronic gadgetry with music. The sequence with the Moog synthesizer grated, despite some delightful Streisand humor. And the appliance sequence failed miserably, with mere noise diverting us from Barbra's singing of a pleasant tune.

Barbra herself gave a magnificent performance, thus making the assorted noises all the more insufferable. Her voice, which has tended to be lost amid over-mechanization on her recent albums, came across as the thing of beauty and purity it is. She had never sounded better—and she indeed used her voice as a musical instrument, making it do wondrous things, hitting notes which sometimes took the viewer's breath away. But the great beauty being projected by Barbra Streisand's voice box was in too many cases destroyed by the gimmickry around her.

The critical reaction to Barbra's fifth special was largely negative, and indicates that Barbra's subsequent specials should be more conventional—not less imaginative, but certainly less damaging to the central purpose of a Barbra Streisand television special: to hear Barbra sing.

Barbra's future in television is uncertain. She will do more specials, but on an irregular basis. She may do guest stints, but rarely and only for friends, such as Burt Bacharach. Will she ever do a series? When she signed with CBS in 1964, she explained that their original concept had indeed been for a series, but that she preferred to do specials; she didn't want the grind associated with a weekly show. Whether she will change her mind depends on the course her career takes. Many big stars turn to television when their movie stock begins to dip. If that does turn out to be the case with Barbra, it is safe to say it will not happen in the near future.

Rehearsing "Sweet Inspiration" for the special.

Barbra and the assembled cast of Barbra Streisand... And
Other Musical Instruments.

SPECIAL GUEST STAR...BARBRA STREISAND!

BOB HOPE SHOW, 1963—With Dean Martin and Bob.

Singing "Gotta Move" on The Bob Hope Show.

THE JUDY GARLAND SHOW, 1963—With Ethel Merman and Judy.

The medley with Judy.

GARRY MOORE SHOW, 1963 — With Carol Burnett, Robert Goulet and Garry.

Judy singing "Be My Guest"

THE BURT BACHARACH SHOW, 1971— "Close To You"

"Be Aware"

MY NAME IS BARBRA
A Columbia Broadcasting System Presentation
April 28, 1965

CREDITS

A VARIETY SPECIAL STARRING BARBRA STREISAND.
PRESENTED BY ELLBAR PRODUCTIONS, INC.
EXECUTIVE PRODUCER: MARTIN ERLICHMAN.
PRODUCED BY RICHARD LEWINE.
DIRECTED BY DWIGHT HEMION.
ASSOCIATE PRODUCER: WILLARD LEVITAS.
MONOLOGUE BY ROBERT EMMETT.
PRODUCTION NUMBERS CONCEIVED BY JOE LAYTON.
ASSISTANT PRODUCER: PEGGY LIEBER.
MUSIC ARRANGED AND CONDUCTED BY PETER MATZ.
PRODUCTION SUPERVISOR: PAUL SHIERS.
ASSOCIATE DIRECTOR: EARL DAWSON.
TECHNICAL DIRECTOR: CARL SCHUTZMAN.
AUDIO SUPERVISOR: B. A. TAYLOR.
LIGHTING DIRECTOR: ROBERT BARRY.
SET DECORATION: BILL HARP.
GRAPHICS: SAM CECERE.
HAIR STYLING BY FREDERICK GLASER.
AUDIO CONSULTANT: FRANK LAICO.
ASSISTANT CONDUCTOR: WILLIAM GOLDENBERG.

PROGRAM OF SONGS

My Name is Barbra
I'm Late
Much More
Lover, Come Back to Me
How Does the Wine Taste?
Make Believe
A Kid Again/I'm Five
Sweet Zoo
Where is the Wonder?
Why Did I Choose You?
People
When the Sun Comes Out
Second Hand Rose
Medley: Second Hand Rose,
    Give Me the Simple Life, I Got Plenty
    of Nothin', Brother Can You Spare
    a Dime?, Nobody Knows You When You're
    Down and Out, The Best Things in Life
    Are Free.
All That I Want
I Am Woman
Don't Rain on My Parade
The Music That Makes
    Me Dance
My Man
Happy Days Are Here Again

"How Does The Wine Taste?"

Monologue—"Pearl from Istanbul" "*I'm Late*"

"*A Kid Again*"

REVIEWS

"When CBS invested $5,000,000 in signing Barbra Streisand to a ten-year contract there were quite a few raised eyebrows in entertainment circles. That's a lot of money for a relatively untried personality—even in show business, where it's easy come, easy go. Well, last night CBS gave viewers and stockholders a very close look at this golden girl. And the investment seems solid. For the one-time kookie kid from Brooklyn has acquired enough performing class to suggest that her considerable promise may be reaching fruition.

"Surrounded by nothing but stylish sets, lavish props and imaginative production numbers conceived by Joe Layton, Miss Streisand admirably displayed the talents that have won her a wide following and a noisy claque which was very much in evidence yesterday. She raced through 23 songs and a little chatter. Sometimes she was a sultry sensualist in a daring low-cut gown managing to out-Lena Lena Horne in a lament like 'Lover Come Back to Me.' Sometimes she was a pixieish gamin reverting to her homey origin in pigtails and a sailor dress lisping a medley of children's songs which threatened to be too cute for comfort, but soon became appealing under the sheer weight of her enthusiasm.

"Throughout the hour a viewer was struck by all the loving tender care that has gone into creating Barbra Streisand. In five short years Miss Streisand's raw material —a throbbing, pleasant pop voice—has been meticulously nurtured and its possessor marvelously groomed. She is beginning to live up to her reputation as a 'brilliant young star.' "

BARBARA DELATINER,
Newsday

"Destined to hit it big in all media, Barbra Streisand last week notched television to the skein that so far lists recordings and the stage ... It is by now old news that she's an electric performer, superbly gifted of voice and ingenuously charming. What counts on television is how the performer projects beyond the glass of the small home screen, and Miss Streisand burst through as though it were no more a barrier than the footlights of a Broadway stage. Her self-confidence, especially for her years and for one so recently come to stardom, is astounding, and she carries it well. Her songs, no matter who they may have 'belonged' to first, come out pure Streisand, styled as originals and somehow always appropriate for what that Egyptian visage, angular frame and off-centre personality all add up to. ..."

Variety

"This special tried so hard to be different and didn't need to. It had Barbra Streisand. It didn't have color, though, and that will cost points. No young singer ever met a tougher challenge head-on and came off like at the head of a parade. . . . To assess the talents of perhaps the best pop femme singer of the going crop is to use most of the synonyms for great. But she is now more than a singer; she's an entertainer with a shade of whimsey that sets her apart. . . . What control and tonal beauty!"

HELM,
Daily Variety

"I'm Five"

"Barbra Streisand, the delicious, off-beat song stylist, leaped upward in her meteoric and still-rising young career with last night's CBS-TV special, *My Name Is Barbra*. More than incidentally, she also put on a rattling good show. The songs, as always, were hand-picked with great care. They were ballads and novelties arranged with cliché-breaking fastidiousness, wholly taken over by the star, shaped to her dramatic, impish and self-kidding style and belted or whispered from a viable music box as if they were just invented. Every number was a performance—from the opening 'Much More' to the closing melancholy 'Happy Days Are Here Again.'"

JOHN HORN,
New York Herald Tribune

"Now consider this girl Barbra Streisand. A gawky 23-year-old gamin, and not a good looker, she has the force of a bulldozer and, at times, the stridency of an ambulence siren. But she's the sensation of Broadway and of the recording industry. Last night in her first special, she gave CBS-TV viewers a full hour of herself.

"In this ultra-expensive, long-touted and eagerly-awaited show . . . the star proved herself to be one of those performers, like Judy Garland, around whom cults are built. Also, she came over as a performer who arouses violently contradictory reactions. A segment of the public regards her as one who over-emotionalizes her numbers sometimes to the embarrassing point of mawkishness. Others worship at her shrine with a fervor and shrill devotion reserved only for the goddesses of song.

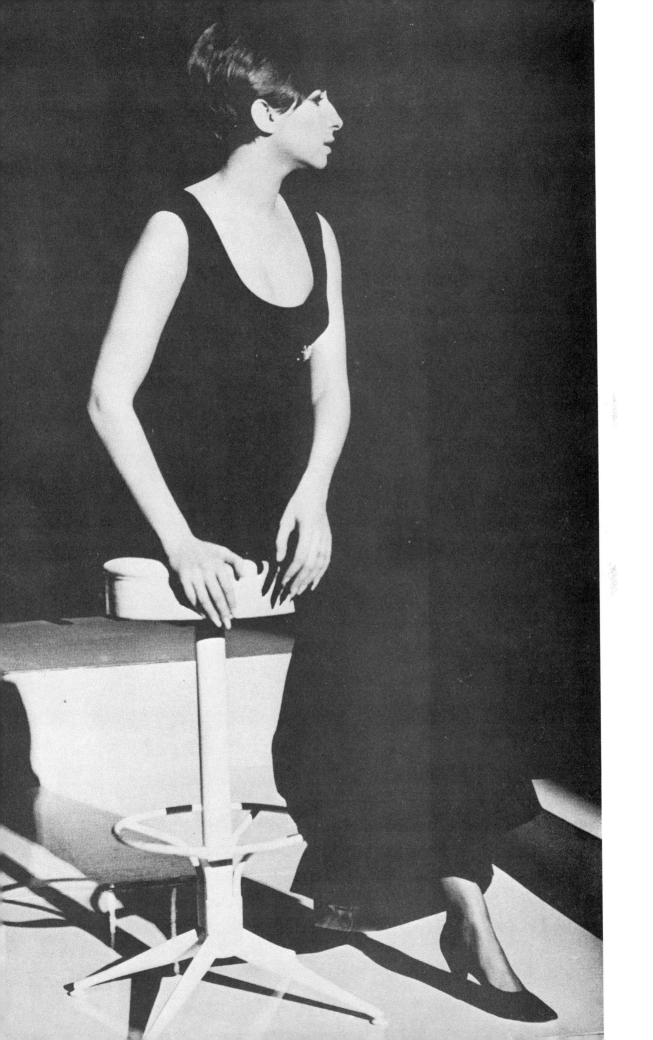

"As far as this viewer is concerned, Barbra is a dynamic performer who literally hurls herself into her number. . . . But she is also one who, in great part, is inclined to stay within the same emotional range. . . . Her voice? By no means a great one. Her acting ability? Fair. But perhaps it's that Barbra has the old Judy Garland-Fanny Brice type of emotionalism which sweeps all before . No doubt about Barbra's draw as a TV attraction, but let's hope her next special will have more variety."

BEN GROSS,
New York Daily News

"Barbra Streisand's first solo spectacular for CBS television was an event more eagerly anticipated than enthusiastically applauded. The after-effect, in fact, was somewhat comparable to finding yourself unable to cash a certified check. After all, we all knew Barbra was an extraordinary talent even before we heard her sing a note. How did we know? Not because of one bad Broadway show or two or three fair record albums, but because the publicists and columnists had spoon-fed us with oily press releases to the effect that everyone was simply enthralled by Barbra.

"Barbra comes on too strong for my taste. . . . It is no secret by now that the Trojan War was not fought on her behalf, and that she looks and talks like somebody's unmarried sister on the loose in the Borscht Belt. Some of her admirers have gone so far as to claim that Barbra is going to put plastic surgeons out of business, which reminds me of the time not so long ago when Audrey Hepburn was going to put bosoms out of business. There is the matter of Barbra's nose, you see, and how much integrity it took for her to keep it as it is. I don't mind her keeping it; it's her flaunting it as the latest Paris style that I find peculiar. Edith Piaf and Helen Morgan were never the comeliest chantoosies in the world, but they didn't flaunt their plainness. They endured it, and then transcended it. They didn't have to mock beauty as an out thing, because they were less concerned with what was in and out that with what was inside and outside."

The Village Voice

"The result was a pinnacle moment in American show business, in any form, in any period. She is so great it is shocking, something like being in love . . . She may well be the most supremely talented and complete popular entertainer that this country has ever produced. She simply dwarfs such contemporary stars as Julie Andrews, Elizabeth Taylor, Judy Garland and Carol Burnett. Anything they can do, she can do light years better. She is alternately gamin-like, sexy, mischievous, innocent, confident, insouciant, girlish, and radiating warmth. So she touches you, to your toes. And then she knocks you out."

United Press International

NOTES

Barbra's first television special was a spectacular success, garnering very high ratings and five Emmy Awards. In addition to her songs, Barbra performed a comic monologue ("Pearl from Istanbul") and chatted with the audience ("I can't believe this is my own show!" she said at one point, and at another told the audience, "There's a play on Broadway, *Funny Girl*. I kind of like it. In fact, I go there every evening.")

At the beginning of the *I'm Five* segment, in which Barbra cavorts in a hugely oversized playground, children begin yelling distantly, "Crazy Barbra . . . Crazy Barbra!" Shades of Barbra's childhood in Brooklyn, no doubt. At the end of *I'm Five*, Barbra gives a birthdate—August 29th. On the recording of *My Name Is Barbra* she changes it to her own, April 24th.

That album and its sequel, *My Name Is Barbra, Two* contain several songs which were not in the original telecast, and leave out several which were. Those omitted were primarily songs previously recorded by Barbra.

In the Philadelphia Museum

COLOR ME BARBRA
A Columbia Broadcasting System Presentation
March 30, 1966

CREDITS

A VARIETY SPECIAL STARRING BARBRA STREISAND.
EXECUTIVE PRODUCER: MARTIN ERLICHMAN.
PRODUCED BY JOE LAYTON AND DWIGHT HEMION.
CONCEIVED AND CHOREOGRAPHED BY JOE LAYTON.
SETS DESIGNED BY TOM JOHN.
DIRECTED BY DWIGHT HEMION.
PRESENTED BY ELLBAR PRODUCTIONS, INC.

PROGRAM OF SONGS

Draw Me a Circle
Yesterdays
One Kiss
The Minute Waltz
Gotta Move

Non C'est Rien
Where or When?
Medley: Animal Crackers in My Soup,
  Funny Face, That Face, They Didn't
  Believe Me, Were Thine That Special
  Face, I've Grown Accustomed to Her
  Face, Let's Face the Music and Dance,
  Sam, You Made the Pants Too Long,
  What's New Pussycat?, Who's Afraid
  of the Big, Bad Wolf, Small World,
  Try to Remember, I Love You,
  I Stayed Too Long at The Fair,
  Look at That Face
C'est Si Bon
Any Place I Hang My Hat is Home
It Had To Be You
Where Am I Going?
Starting Here, Starting Now

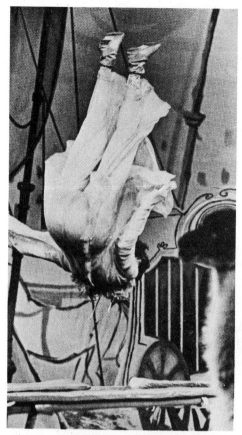

The Circus Sequence

REVIEWS

"Barbra Streisand's success on her first hour-long special was no lucky accident. She proved that last night when, in *Color Me Barbra*, her second annual appearance on the Columbia Broadcasting System, she did variations on the formula of her first show and, if anything, topped herself.

"This does not mean that Miss Streisand was the constant focus of attention. Few guests could have upstaged her quite as successfully as some of her associates in the circus sequence—an anteater with whom she rubbed profiles, a baby elephant who offered her a welcoming trunk and some penguins who stomped around in their natural dress suits while Miss Streisand sang, 'Sam, You Made the Pants Too Long.'

"At the Philadelphia Museum, Miss Streisand kept herself more prominently in the picture, quite literally. Wandering through long halls and labyrinthine rooms while she sang, she took her cues from paintings, from tapestries and from sculpture. She became the Egyptian Nefertiti, a Modigliani girl singing at a cafe table, and Marie Antionette trying to complete a vocal version of *The Minute Waltz* in the shadow of the guillotine.

"In color, the museum settings were magnificent, the circus was happy and Miss Streisand looked gorgeous. It was a fun show—free and easy when it might have been pretentious, disarming when it might have turned coy."

JOHN S. WILSON,
The New York Times

"It was a haunting voice, harsh and yet at times soft, like a distant wail filled with inexpressible longing. Singing 'Draw Me a Circle,' Barbra Streisand launched her second special. . . . It was a virtuoso effort, an impressive one-woman show. Those who are not Streisand worshippers perhaps found a complete hour devoted to her songs lacking in variety. But the men and women, boys and girls who are Streisand aficionadoes could not get enough of her talent . . . in this top song show of the season. Actually, Barbra was the whole show. She could have held her audience on a bare stage with one tinkling piano."

BEN GROSS,
New York Daily News

"With imagination, ingenuity and most of all Miss Streisand herself, this *Color Me Barbra* emerged this past Wednesday evening as a stunning, colorful and enormously exciting venture. The only human figure on view was Miss Streisand. . . . It is indicative of the quality of the program that even under such circumstances, even with only Miss Streisand on view . . . the hour seemed to go by all too quickly, leaving you at the end sitting there and wishing for some more . . . it takes a great personality, as well as a first-rate singer, to hold a TV show on the sheer strength of her own talents. Barbra Streisand did it magnificently in *Color Me Barbra*. It's difficult to see how any other television musical show can top it for the rest of the year. Unless, of course, a third Barbra Streisand program is to be scheduled."

LEO MISHKIN,
New York Morning Telegraph

"Barbra Streisand must be a lousy golfer. Why? Because nobody can be all good. She can sing, dance, act, grace stylish clothing or outlandish duds, look beautiful with the short change nature gave her, convince viewers she's a child or a femme fatale, show a sense of humor, even about herself, and she likes animals. I know from the years she spent with mother and living by herself she had to learn something about cooking. But everybody has a weakness and I figure hers must be golf.

"Which is the long way of saying Barbra teed off on her second television special . . . A fine hour of entertainment and one which, while not aimed at children, was wholesome enough for them to watch. . . . In the third portion, Barbra again closed out in a stand-up concert before a studio audience. Her voice sounds richer than ever, if that's possible. And considering her still tender years, it is. One Streisand a year won't make a TV season, but it certainly will be awaited eagerly, for its glow will last long beyond anything television provides as regular fare."

AL SALERNO,
New York World-Telegram and Sun

"For Barbra Streisand's second spec of the season, CBS delivered a true one-woman turn—not another biped in sight the whole hour distance. As it turned out, the exercise in conceit was justified, credit as much Joe Layton's tasteful staging as the star's own talents and singular personality. It's pretty obvious the femme can carry the load. Miss Streisand's normal propensity is to line out each and every number with emotion full tilt, even if, in the prime of her youth, its hard to imagine deep past sufferings. At any rate, this time out she varied the intensity a bit, and definitely for the better. . . ."

Variety

THE BELLE OF 14th STREET
A Columbia Broadcasting System Presentation
October 11, 1967

CREDITS

PRESENTED BY ELLBAR PRODUCTIONS, INC.
EXECUTIVE PRODUCER: MARTIN ERLICHMAN.
PRODUCED BY JOE LAYTON.
DIRECTED BY JOE LAYTON AND WALTER C.
MILLER.
SCRIPT BY ROBERT EMMETT.
COSTUMES BY FRED VOELPEL.
MUSIC ARRANGED AND CONDUCTED BY MORT
LINDSAY.

CAST

BARBRA STREISAND, JASON ROBARDS, JOHN
BUBBLES, LEE ALLEN. BEEF TRUST GIRLS: MARY
ALICE VOELKLE, BARBARA TERRY, PATTY SAUERS,
HARRIET GIBSON, NORMA DAVIDS, CAROL
SWANBERG

PROGRAM OF SONGS

I'm Always Chasing Rainbows
Put Your Arms Around Me, Honey
Some of These Days
Happy Days Are Here Again
Alice Blue Gown
Liebestraum
Mother Machree
I Don't Care
Melancholy Baby
My Buddy
How About Me?
A Good Man Is Hard to Find
We're Four Americans
Apple of My Eye
I'm Going South
Nobody But Me

"We're Four Americans" (with Jason Robards)

REVIEWS

"Barbra Streisand's third television special ... was an embarrassing outing, a concoction of deranged productions that not even the star and her major colleague of the evening, Jason Robards, could straighten out. Since Miss Streisand last summer filled Central Park at a concert, her popularity hardly could be questioned, but last night she seemed far more concerned with superfluous melodramatic gestures than with the genuine emotional meaning of the lyrics she was singing. For all the diversity of her selections, they sounded disconcertingly similar, and musically the hour never achieved a semblance of inspiration. Miss Streisand needs much more careful guidance in what to do than she received.

"The central theme of *The Belle of 14th Street* was theoretically a nostalgic throwback to the turn of the century. ... Whatever his stature on the legitimate stage, Mr. Robards is no song and dance man, and his opening number with a beef-trust chorus was a total and tasteless disaster. ... *The Belle of 14th Street* obviously reflected the producer's concern that the show's idea could not stand on its own and needed additional modern gimmickry. The consequence was to raise the question of what a network means by the phrase 'a special.'"

JACK GOULD,
The New York Times

"Barbra Streisand's third CBS-TV special, an attempt to recreate America's turn-of-the-century vaudeville grind, lost something in the video transition. But the femme herself still registered as a personal triumph, and almost managed thereby to salvage the hour from ho-humsville. ... The enterprise seemed to have satire high in mind, but the effort was spottily effective. One of the sharper tacks, involving some electronic wizardry, was the running two-Streisands bit. In one number, the star as an on-stage diva was joined by the star from a box seat, just like in the flicks.

"In the show's latter half, it was Streisand solo lining out the musichall oldies as la Belle of 14th Street, and it was this segment in which the production—and its star—came off best. It's something of a show just digging the close-ups of that personalized Streisand mugg. At least part of the admiration is for the fact that she's resisted all that nose bob advice."

Variety

The diva sings "Liebestraum"

"Mother Machree"

Ariel flies

Ferdinand and Miranda of "The Tempest" (with Jason Robards)

"The third annual TV 'special' of stylish songstress Barbra Streisand on CBS last night was nothing to be compared with her previous solo ventures on the home screen, which won so much applause . . . Miss Streisand functioned much better alone, in her two previous solos, than she did with the help of actor Jason Robards, vaudevillian John Bubbles and an unsightly 'beef trust' chorus. She was less than winning with German and Irish accents in some of the questionable numbers, but she came to life late in the hour singing—and being—herself, emphasized nose and all. The camera gimmicks this time almost defeated the strangely attractive girl."

BOB WILLIAMS,
New York Post

"What could have been a dynamic, pungent hour, Barbra Streisand's special *The Belle of 14th Street* came across as a mere mild venture into nostalgia on CBS-TV last night. It was most of the time a likeable enough entertainment with an old but appealing basic idea. However, it lacked the impact one has a right to expect of a vehicle on which a superstar tries to ride to glory. . . . To her aficionados, nothing matters as long as Barbra is in front of the camera. In all truth, it must be recorded, in a wide list of numbers ranging from *Liebestraum* and *Alice Blue Gown* to *My Melancholy Baby* and *I'm Always Chasing Rainbows*, she was better than ever before on TV. Her small but distinctive voice and her delivery have a magical quality for her devoted worshippers.

"Save for the time when Barbra held the stage alone and delivered a truly effective group of songs, the hour had a consciously coy and artificial air about it. This segment was the highlight of the show. For without gimmickry, it offered pure undiluted Streisand and showed her at her best."

BEN GROSS,
New York Daily News

"In her two earlier specials, Barbra Streisand was center stage, in what commonly is called a one-woman show. This time around, even with helpers, it was sti[ll] solo performance. While she and the camera stared at ea[ch] other, the hour passed with abandon in the old New Y[ork] fashion. The others filled to let her catch her breath . [. .] The *Tempest* skit with Robards didn't enhance the sho[w] musical flavor but did permit Miss Streisand to fly [on] wires a la Peter Pan. There were many lapses of her o[wn] patented styling on several numbers but the magic of [her] voice still carried her to the heights reached by few of t[he] current canary crop. Not one to parade her figure, she [did] a strip in a break-away gown that added novelty to [an] otherwise music fest."

HEL[?]
Daily Varie[ty]

"Worshippers at the shrine of Barbra Streisand, w[ho] must number in the millions by now, must have had a f[ine] time with the third of the special TV programs given ov[er] to her art . . . officially known as *The Barbra Streisa[nd] Special*, the hour, . . . as a foretaste of what might [be] expected from Miss Streisand's two forthcoming moti[on] pictures, *Funny Girl* and *Hello, Dolly!*, put her back i[n] the costumes, the atmosphere, and a dozen or so so[ng] numbers of 30 to 50 years ago. She looked, it may [be] added, simply elegant in every one of them. And sa[ng] good, too.

"But it was not only Barbra Streisand who made [up] the show. Jason Robards, a celebrated dramatic actor, wi[th] experience in Eugene O'Neill, Shakespeare and *A Tho[u]sand Clowns*, among other things, made his official deb[ut] on the program as a singing and performing partner . [. .] One of the high points of the hour, indeed, had M[iss] Robards and Miss Streisand playing excerpts from Shak[e]speare's *The Tempest* with Miss Streisand playing bo[th] Ariel and Miranda, with Robards as Prospero, Prince Fe[r]dinand, and even Caliban, in an enormous monkey su[it.] That you couldn't hear the Shakespearean poetry ve[ry] well, and that both of these people put on outrageous pe[r]formances, fit very nicely into the scheme of things."

LEO MISHKI[N]
New York Morning Telegra[ph]

"Alice Blue Gown"

A HAPPENING IN CENTRAL PARK
A Columbia Broadcasting System Presentation
September 16, 1968

CREDITS

A MUSICAL SPECIAL STARRING BARBRA STREISAND.
PRODUCED AND DIRECTED BY ROBERT SCHEERER.
EXECUTIVE PRODUCER MARTIN ERLICHMAN.
MONOLOGUE BY BOB HILLIARD.
LIGHTING BY IMERO FIORENTINO.
STAGED BY TOM JOHN.
MUSICAL DIRECTION BY MORT LINDSAY.

PROGRAM OF SONGS

The Nearness of You
Down With Love
New Love Is Like a Newborn Child
Cry Me A River
Folk Monologue
I Can See It
Love Is a Bore
He Touched Me
English Folksong
I'm All Smiles
Marty the Martian
Natural Sounds
Second Hand Rose
People
Silent Night
Happy Days Are Here Again

REVIEWS

"A tape recording of Barbra Streisand's one-woman concert in Central Park in June, 1967, finally reached the home screen last night in a special over the network of the Columbia Broadcasting System. Compared with her previous television appearances, Miss Streisand has improved both in stage presence and in her selection of songs . . . Even if Miss Streisand's popularity is not to be disputed, there may be a few, one of whom happens to be this viewer, who feel that still more time may be required for the realization of her full potential. Intuitively, she is aware of the importance of changing emotional moods in an hour-long concert, but in her singing the contrast has not yet come to the surface.

"Her phrasing is all of a pattern, and the ability to achieve that inflection of mood, that penetration of the true meaning of a set of lyrics, remains to be realized. The tip-off comes in the immobility of her eyes, which so often are the most accurate mirror of what a singer is thinking. . . . Because Miss Streisand as yet is not a finished singer in the musical sense, when she is not careful, a monotone creeps into her work, and after an hour the uncommitted viewer may have left the program with a feeling that somehow she made a great many different numbers sound disconcertingly similar.

"But it may well be that this is a shortcoming of such a viewer rather than of Miss Streisand. In the modern genre there is a coolness beneath the emotion of the songs she prefers. When she manages the difficult task of conveying a sense of warm feeling without excessive bodily gyrations, she may easily win over those who for the moment have reservations. That she can display continuing growth amid all the burdens of immediate stardom is an encouraging omen."

JACK GOULD,
The New York Times

"It was about time last night, after 15 months, that CBS finally aired its dusty videotape of Barbra Streisand's Central Park concert ... it was surprising how pleasantly the old program registered in the living room, however, without the customarily false trappings of the usual studio-staged 'special.' The camera captured Miss Streisand communicating with the vast assemblage of fans in a videotaped show which might better have been played by CBS in a June, July or August night more appropriate to the original hot-weather occasion. As it turned out, however, it didn't matter. The evening was a winning one."

BOB WILLIAMS,
New York Post

"It's not easy to sing your heart out before 128,000 fans and achieve a quality of intimacy under the stars in the stately wide open greenery of Central Park. But Miss Streisand managed it in a remarkable performance of spontaneity and assurance Sunday night during which she played that vast audience like a tuned-up violin. There were seventeen numbers in various tempos—upbeat and slow, ballad and comedy, delivered in a sylvan setting by a soaring bird in diaphanous flowing gowns. This was truly a 'happening'—a rapport between entertainer and entertained that could be shared by millions—thanks to the magic of videotape."

PERCY SHAIN,
Boston Globe

". . . A night on which Barbra was in excellent voice made her 'happening' a triumph. Her material was tasty, her lower Second Avenue Kook City image was held to a minimum of adlibbing, and the television audience saw only the best of the evening. Highlights: some beautiful helicopter shots of New York after dark, Barbra doing a delightful reprise of one of her earliest underground hits, 'I'm In Love With Harold Mingert,' a lovely arrangement of 'Silent Night,' and Barbra cradling the mob in the palm of her hand with two hair-raisingly beautiful new songs— 'New Love Is Like a Newborn Child' and 'Natural Sounds.' Thrilling."

REX REED

"Barbra Streisand, showing absolutely no Soul and to all appearances quite satisfied about it, proved once more with her special . . . she has reached a category reserved for very few entertainers: superstardom. With polished control, she played her audience's emotions with cocksure

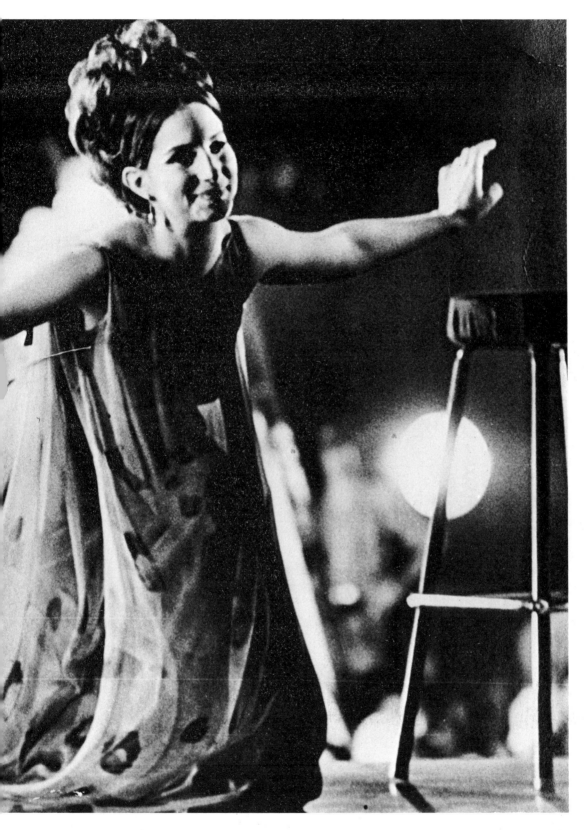

ing and projection . . . For the home audience, the act remains ambivalent. Appreciating the high style technical brilliance of the show itself, the viewer can be worn out by Miss Streisand's manipulated intensity, noved by the lingering close-ups every time she goes and slow and dramatic. But a Streisand special is quite special, indeed, and merits watching. It undoubtedly was, as the Nielson count should attest. . . . Miss Streisand ran handsomely through her repertoire and rapport. . . . When she is good, she is very, very good."

ESSE,
Daily Variety

BARBRA STREISAND . . . AND OTHER MUSICAL INSTRUMENT

A Columbia Broadcasting System Presentation
November 2, 1973

A MUSICAL SPECIAL STARRING BARBRA STREISAND,
WITH GUEST STAR RAY CHARLES.
PRODUCED BY GARY SMITH AND DWIGHT HEMION,
IN ASSOCIATION WITH JOE LAYTON.
DIRECTED BY DWIGHT HEMION.
EXECUTIVE PRODUCER: MARTIN ERLICHMAN.
MUSICAL MATERIALS WRITTEN AND ARRANGED
BY KEN AND MITZIE WELCH.
DIALOGUE BY LARRY GELBART AND KEN AND
MITZIE WELCH.
CHOREOGRAPHY BY JOE LAYTON.
MUSICAL DIRECTION BY JACK PARNELL.
SOUND DIRECTOR: BILL NUTTALL.
AN ATV PRODUCTION FOR ITC WORLDWIDE
DISTRIBUTION.

PROGRAM OF SONGS

Sing/Make Your Own Kind of Music
Piano Practicing
I Got Rhythm
One Note Samba
Glad to Be Unhappy
People
Second Hand Rose
Don't Rain on My Parade
Don't Ever Leave Me
By Myself
Come Back to Me
Look What They've Done to My Song, Ma.
Cryin' Time
Sweet Inspiration
Auf dem Wasser zu Singen
I Never Has Seen Snow
On a Clear Day You Can See Forever
The World is a Concerto/Make Your
   Own Kind of Music
The Sweetest Sounds

"One Note Samba" (East Indian)

(Above center) With Dominic Savage, the 11-year-old British pianist who accompanied her on "I Got Rhythm." Barbra gave his age as 8.

(Above right) "People" (with Barbra as a Turkish belly dancer)

"I Got Rhythm" (with an African beat)

"The program is well-made, and it certainly is expen-
But it is overproduced, over-orchestrated and over-
ing to the point of esthetic nausea. . . . Taped in
don, the show uses an interesting concept, devised by
y Smith and Dwight Hemion, two of the more tal-
d producers of TV musicals. In a large studio, with
ilevel platforms, the star is reinforced with a full
estra plus a slew of international musicians playing
r national instruments. That much is fine. But what is
osedly meant to be an 'album of international music'
s out to be little more than a labored gimmick. The
ional instruments merely serve as window dressing for
dard Streisand interpretations of standard ballads. . . .
"The best part of the program is grabbed by Ray
rles singing by himself ('Look What They've Done to
Song, Ma') and with Miss Streisand ('Cryin' Time
in'). There are no gimmicks, no echo chambers, no
y camera shots, no fashion magazine posing—just
d music. And it's a relief."

JOHN J. O'CONNOR
The New York Times

"From the moment the songstress sprays her throat
tunes up with Jack Parnell's Orchestra, one senses that
ething out of the ordinary is about to happen. Wear-
a velvet dress with a scooped neckline that plunges as
r as some of the notes she sings, with a bow tie at the
k, and her long tresses swept up in a turn-of-the-cen-
y hairdo, Miss Streisand guides us through a musical
rney that's as exciting as *Alice's Adventures in Won-
land*. Indeed, you get curioser and curioser as this
thmic, imaginative and humorous hour unfolds, domi-
ed, of course, by La Streisand, a consummate performer
brilliant architect of a stellar show business career . . .
ile we would have preferred the hour to end on a
re sentimental note, 'On a Clear Day,' for instance, the
l symphony of daily appliances from washing machines
orange squeezers, and even Singer sewing machines,
ich briefly recall the wild and wooly Spike Jones era, is
ginative and in keeping with the star's feeling for musi-
humor."

KAY GARDELLA,
New York Daily News

"The World is a Concerto" (with vacuum cleaners, electric toothbrushes and Marty Erlichman at the washing ma

"Barbra Streisand has stayed off television for five years—as a matter of personal choice. All that while, CBS has been paying her a goodly sum to keep her non-service exclusive with that network. Last Friday, she finally deigned to give CBS the pleasure of her company. Whether it was worth the wait depends largely on whether one is an admirer of the lady. There was certainly nothing in the special to indicate that she wants to change anyone's mind about how they feel about her. Her selection of songs was right out of her—by now—old bag of standards, keyed to the middle-class middle-brows where she has always found her deepest admiration.

"While it would be difficult to fault Streisand's voice, it is less difficult to fault her human quality—it is sorely lacking. She turns herself on, but she manipulates a song rather than sings it. . . . The production in London, under the aegis of Independent Television Corp., was first-rate. Largely concocted out of lighting and other effects, it was colorful and opulent looking. The many changes of handsome costumes also added some color to the proceedings.

"The singer also essayed some dance steps during the performance, and she would be well-advised in the future to keep that sort of thing at a minimum. She was just plain clumsy."

FOB,
Variety

HENRY GROS

PART FOUR / Movies

With Omar Sharif during Funny Girl *filming*

When Barbra Streisand arrived in Hollywood in May 1967 for the filming of the Ray Stark movie version of *Funny Girl*, she was a superstar of Broadway, records, and television. The only entertainment frontier she had yet to conquer was the legendary tinsel-town and, as Barbra told a reporter as she disembarked from her flight, "being a star is being a *movie* star."

Few observers doubted that Barbra would complete a grand slam of the entertainment media, and from the start she was treated like old-time filmdom royalty. She was invited to all the parties, featured in all the gossip columns and pursued by star-gazers, reporters, photographers and fans. It was a beautiful honeymoon, but it lasted only until the first few days of shooting.

By that time, the columnists were reporting, Barbra, who had yet to prove herself in films, was acting like all the classic temperamental Hollywood prima donnas before her. Reports emanating from the *Funny Girl* set told of Barbra trying to produce, direct and photograph as well as star in her first film. She was said to be treating Academy Award-winning director William Wyler like "a butler," insisting on doing over scenes he found entirely satisfactory, and telling another Oscar winner, cinematographer Harry Stradling, how to light her. She reportedly insisted on either Gregory Peck or Marlon Brando to play Nicky Arnstein, and finally "gave in" and "approved" Omar Sharif.

She was said to have stormed off the set on several occasions when disputes arose, to have spent hours by herself incommunicado, and to have insisted on complete veto power over all her photographs.

The reports made marvelous gossip as Barbra was painted as a real, live girl monster. But before long her director, and finally Barbra herself began coming to her defense. William Wyler, when asked if he found it "difficult" to work with Streisand, said "Barbra is very interesting to work with. Not easy and not difficult. She is completely wrapped up in her work. She's got ideas on how to perform. Some are good, some are not good. Ten times I would rather have somebody like her. An actor has got to use his head as well as his body."

Some members of the cast and crew, however, didn't take so kindly to Barbra's perfectionism. They resented her demands for retakes and scene changes, and they blamed her for almost all production problems which arose. Anne Francis, when her part as Georgia was cut, blamed Streisand; Barbra protested that when the Broadway show needed trimming, that role was the first to be cut: it wasn't her fault if the part was expendable. Barbra also sought to explain some of the hard feelings between star and crew: "Once, I said to Wyler that I would like to record a song live instead of dubbing it in later as it's usually done in movies. Wyler couldn't have been more pleased. But I suppose some of the people on the set could have seen this and said, 'She's making trouble.' They're not used to actors talking up in Hollywood."

riving in Hollywood with Elliot and Jason, May 1967.

With Ray Stark and Herb Ross during Funny Girl *filming.*

With Jason on Funny Girl *set*

While Barbra was being portrayed in the press as the temperamental ading lady, the gossips were also envisioning another classic Hollywood adition: the romance between the star and her leading man. It was erfect: the former homely Brooklyn Jewish girl and the dashingly andsome Arab playboy. When Barbra and Omar Sharif hit it off after eir first meeting, the gossips' tongues began wagging furiously, and hen the couple spent hours together in Barbra's dressing room, the olumnists could hardly contain their delight. The first on-set kiss etween the two was wire-photoed across the globe and created a furor in gypt: Cairo's leading newspaper ran a front-page editorial condemning harif for associating with a Jewess. Barbra, told of this, quipped, "You hink Cairo was upset? You should have seen the letter I got from my unt Rose!" Sharif dismissed the controversy with aplomb. "I've never sked a girl her nationality before kissing her," he said.

The talk of a romance between Streisand and Sharif continued to pread, and was hardly dampened when Omar was quoted in *Life* as aying, "When I first saw Barbra, I am thinking, 'This is not a pretty woman.' But in three days, I am thinking, 'This woman is beautiful.' And am *lusting* after her." Barbra was reported as saying, "I'm crazy in love with Omar and I have told my Elliot about it." Back in New York, Gould blasted the gossips for spreading false reports. "I love her and trust her all he way," he told Sheila Graham.

Whatever it was between Omar and Barbra, it was over soon after he filming. Hollywood, however, was grateful for great copy while it asted. Now, with no more romance and no more temper tantrums to eport, the columnists began leaking information about Barbra's per-

At New York party following Funny Girl *opening.*

formance. They told of her debut as a ballerina in a parody of *Swan L*, her ride on a tugboat past the Statue of Liberty and her heart-rending version of "My Man" at the film's finale. The word was out that Barbra performance was great, the film was a sure hit, and Barbra was on the threshold of Hollywood superstardom.

When *Funny Girl* was released, Streisand's performance created a sensation rarely equaled in Hollywood history. Reviewers were ecstatic Rex Reed called it "the most remarkable screen debut I will probably e see in my lifetime." Joseph Morgenstern of *Newsweek* called Streisand performance "the most accomplished, original and enjoyable musical comedy performance ever put on film." While the movie itself met wit mixed reaction, Barbra was unanimously hailed. Her position as a star i the great Hollywood tradition could hardly be questioned.

Funny Girl shattered the popular conception of Barbra Streisand a an "ugly duckling." Moviegoers were amazed at how beautiful she lool in portions of the film, and Barbra's childhood dream had now come totally true. She knew it was all real one day when she received a letter "I just got a note from Hedy Lamarr, one of the most beautiful women the world . . . she said I made Elizabeth Taylor look like an old bag. . . ."

The New York premiere of *Funny Girl* was another chapter straig from the golden days of Hollywood. Barbra stopped traffic as she cross Broadway on a red carpet to enter the Criterion Theatre amid thousand of cheering fans. The only thing left for Barbra now to cement her plac in the upper echelon of stardom was that glittering symbol of excellenc and popularity, the legendary Oscar. She had already won awards for h Broadway performances, television specials and recordings, as well as a Golden Globe for *Funny Girl*. Could she make a clean sweep of the awards in all media?

When the nominations were announced in February 1969, Barbra v indeed cited, but so too were Katharine Hepburn, for her acclaimed performance in *The Lion in Winter*, Patricia Neal, for her touching and miraculous comeback in *The Subject Was Roses*, Vanessa Redgrave in *Isadora* and Joanne Woodward in *Rachel, Rachel*. Each of Barbra's competitors was a star of experience and stature, and each had given a superb performance. Could Barbra, in her first film, beat out all these veterans? When she arrived at the ceremonies on the evening of April 1 1969, the air was tense and excited. Elliot Gould stood by his nervous wife, lending her moral support through the excruciating wait until the announcement was made.

Finally, the next-to-last winner of the evening was to be named. When Ingrid Bergman opened the envelope containing the name of the Best Actress of 1968, she gasped. "It's a tie!" she cried in amazement, an as the crowd held its breath, she went on. "The *winners* are . . . Katharir Hepburn . . ."—there was applause and heightened anticipation—"and . . Barbra Streisand!" The crowd burst into cheers as Barbra, beaming with joy and excitement, went up to accept Hollywood's ultimate accolade. After an acceptance speech was made for Katharine Hepburn, Barbra toasted the great star by saying, "I'm honored to be in such magnificent company." She then held up the statuette, looked at it and exclaimed, "Hello, Gorgeous!"—a reference to her opening line in *Funny Girl*. At that moment, Barbra was at the very top, and she was basking in the acclaim of her colleagues.

The announcement of Barbra's next film raised quite a few eyebrow in Hollywood. For years, the show *Hello, Dolly!* had represented competition for Barbra Streisand. It and *Funny Girl* were the two major shows to open on Broadway in 1964, and immediately *Hello, Dolly!*

opped the lion's share of the limelight. It won nine Tony Awards, including Best Musical and, for Carol Channing, Best Musical Actress, an award Barbra undoubtedly coveted. While *Funny Girl* closed after three years, *Hello, Dolly!* went on to set the all-time record for Broadway performances.

Thus, it came as quite a surprise to Barbra when she was asked to play the Dolly role in the 20th Century-Fox film version of the play. She certainly did not fit the image everyone had of Dolly Gallagher Levi: a meddlesome, middle-aged widow. Was Barbra, scarcely twenty-six, going to wear aging make-up? "I thought they were kidding," she says. "I didn't want to do it. I told them not to hire me." But the film's producer, Ernest Lehman, was persistent, and explained, "I'm not implying criticism of anyone else who has done the role previously, but I chose Miss Streisand because I'm convinced she's one of the most exciting talents to come along in the recent past and I know she'll be perfect for the role."

Hollywood observers, however, were cynical. They saw Lehman's move as purely commercial, an attempt to cash in at the box office on the excitement which surrounded Barbra Streisand. There was a great deal of resentment when Barbra's signing was announced. Most people in the business felt that Carol Channing, who had just been nominated for a Supporting Actress Oscar for her role in *Thoroughly Modern Millie*, should be given the opportunity to re-create the role she originated. Channing, however, took it graciously. After sending Barbra flowers and congratulations, she told a reporter, "I'm really very glad that Barbra Streisand got it. Obviously, with Barbra being so different from me, they're going to do a completely different kind of story and it should be very exciting."

Despite Miss Channing's apparent lack of animosity, resentment accompanied Barbra to the *Dolly* set. The gossip about Streisand's working habits on this film was even worse than that which had come from the *Funny Girl* soundstage. She was frequently reported storming off the set in a huff, and having open fights with director Gene Kelly and co-star Walter Matthau. There was definitely no love lost between Matthau and Barbra. They frequently quarrelled, and crew members were quick to report the details to a waiting public. At one point, when Barbra was making a suggestion to Gene Kelly, Matthau said acidly, "Why don't you let the director direct?" Barbra shot back: "Why don't you learn your lines?" Another time, Barbra criticized an aspect of Matthau's acting technique. "Cool it, baby," Walter growled. "You may be the singer in this picture, but I'm the actor."

As further reports amplified Barbra's reputation as a terror, she again found herself defending her actions. "I want good performances around me," she said. "I'm not just interested in my performance. I'm interested in props, the fabric of my dress—it all affects my performance." All Walter Matthau could manage was the admission that "Barbra has moments of likeability. . . ."

Hello, Dolly!, for all its spectacular success on Broadway, became a jinxed movie. It went tremendously over budget, and finally wound up being the most expensive movie musical ever made, costing somewhere between twenty and twenty-five million dollars. Once it was finished, a legal battle over the film's release ensued between 20th Century-Fox and David Merrick, the show's Broadway producer. In 1964, when the contract to film *Dolly* was signed, a stipulation stated that the movie version could not be released until after the show closed or January 1971, whichever came first. Since no one expected the show to run seven years, little thought was given to the clause. But due to Merrick's showmanship,

Talking with Princess Margaret at London Funny Girl *premiere (With Omar Sharif)*

Fighting her way through the crowd at New York premiere of Hello, Dolly!

Barbra strikes an appropriate pose after being named to the International Best Dressed List in 1969.

At the New York Dolly *premiere with Louis Armstrong.*

primarily in giving *Dolly* an all-Black cast headed by Pearl Bailey, the show was still running in late 1969, when the film was ready for release. After months of legal hassle, Merrick relented when 20th agreed to reimburse him for any business lost because of the movie's competition. The film opened in New York in December, at the Rivoli Theatre.

At the premiere, Barbra experienced her first case of uncontrolled mobism. A thousand fans shoved and pushed their way toward her car and began rocking it back and forth through the sheer force of their numbers. A flying wedge of policemen was formed to get the star from her car to the theater door. Just as she got into the theater, the police barricades collapsed and bedlam broke loose. Barbra was badly shaken and several people were injured, including Marty Erlichman, her manager, who would up with a bloody nose.

Hello, Dolly! proved to be a film hardly on a par with *Funny Girl.* It was widely criticized for unbelievability of plot, nonsensical characters and a cardboard appearance. Barbra's personal notices were better. While some critics noted that her "obvious youth and real sexuality," in the words of Vincent Canby, made the Dolly characterization somewhat incongruous, most felt that Barbra created an enjoyable Dolly and was one of the best things about the movie. Barbra performed many of her less credible scenes with tongue in cheek. At one point, when she is supposedly teaching a fellow to dance we know is a professional dancer, she reacts with mock amazement at his agility and ad libs, "I think he's been holding out on us!"

The film, grand and wholesome entertainment despite its shortcomings, was a popular success, but due entirely to its indefensible budget, it was a financial disaster. Although it has grossed fifteen million dollars to date, as much as *Rosemary's Baby, Little Big Man, This Is Cinerama* and *The Bible,* 20th Century-Fox is still ten million dollars in the red. Barbra has since called the film, "The worst mistake I ever made."

In July 1969, Barbra performed at the opening of Las Vegas' International Hotel, billed as the largest entertainment complex in the world. Rumor had it that Barbra was receiving $100,000 a week for her appearance, and with characteristic irony, she opened her show with "I've Got Plenty of Nothin'." Barbra's first several nights at the International failed to cause the stir which had been expected: she was accused of giving a nonchalant and lackluster performance. Shaken by the criticism, Barbra changed her repertoire, including more songs and less chatter, and began wowing her audience as before. On the whole, the engagement was a success.

The hotel was not quite finished when Barbra's show began. One night, while she was singing "Jingle Bells?," a shower of white flakes began falling from the ceiling. "That's not snow," Barbra told the audience nervously, "that's *plaster.*"

During 1969, Barbra's personal life was in a state of flux. She and Elliot Gould parted in what they termed an "amiable separation." Barbra told a reporter, "We've separated to save our marriage, not destroy it." They never were able to reconcile, however, and were granted a divorce in the Dominican Republic on July 9, 1971. Barbra still speaks kindly of Elliot. In an interview late in 1972, she said of him: "Once you have loved someone, they become part of what you were and therefore part of what you *are.*" After the separation, Elliot became a major star in such movies as *Bob and Carol and Ted and Alice, M*A*S*H* and *Getting Straight.* A relationship with Jennifer Bogart produced two children. During the summer of 1973, rumors began circulating of a reconciliation between Gould and Barbra, but these must have been unfounded, since Elliot and Jennifer were married in December of 1973.

Barbra's own love life was anything but prosaic after her separation from Gould. In January 1970, she journeyed to Ottawa, Canada, to visit Prime Minister Pierre Trudeau, reputed to be a "swinging bachelor." Trudeau and Barbra had dated previously in New York, and he escorted her around Ottawa. She attended a session of Canada's parliament, and Trudeau repeatedly smiled from the floor at Barbra, who was sitting in the visitors' gallery. Finally, George Hess, a member of the opposition party, asked Trudeau to answer a question, "If the Prime Minister can take his eyes and mind off the visitors' gallery long enough to answer." Trudeau smiled and blushed, while Barbra tapped the gallery rail in appreciation.

The couple saw each other several times afterwards, and gossip columnists visualized a torrid romance which would make Barbra Canada's First Lady. If an actual romance did exist, it was long over by the time Trudeau wed Margaret Sinclair on March 5, 1971.

Barbra continued to figure prominently in the news during 1969. She was named the Friars Club's "Entertainer of the Year," only the second woman ever to be so honored by the all-male theatrical organization. She was honored as "Star of the Year" by the National Association of Theatre Owners, and she was voted a special Tony Award as "Star of the Decade."

Toward the end of that eventful year, Barbra made news outside the realm of show business. On December 2, 1969, *The New York Times* reported that Streisand was considering a complaint to the New York City Human Rights Commission over her rejection by a Park Avenue cooperative apartment building. Barbra had attempted to purchase a $240,000, twenty-room apartment and was rejected, she claimed, as part of a systematic discrimination against Jews which was already being investigated at the time. The building manager's wife stated that Streisand was turned down because she was a "flamboyant type." Barbra retorted in a written statement, "I have been criticized in Hollywood for not attending premieres or giving parties. . . . I had thought that the mid-Victorian notion of actors as undesirables or second-class citizens was a prejudice which had gone the way of the bustle. I am an actress by choice; I am proud of my profession, and I am not prepared to accept an infringement on my civil rights because of it."

New York's Attorney General Louis Lefkowitz ordered a special investigation into the matter, but Barbra began looking elsewhere. She finally found a five-story brownstone on Manhattan's East 80th Street, for which she paid between $375,000 and $420,000.

At the 1969 Academy Award ceremonies, Barbra sits anxiously while the list of "Best Actress" nominees is read . . . turns to Elliot in joy as her name is announced . . . and graciously accepts her Oscar.

Barbra began 1970 on a happy professional note, being named *Cue* magazine's "Entertainer of the Year" for the second time. Citing her success in *Funny Girl*, her Academy Award, *Hello, Dolly!*, her Las Vegas appearance, an Ed Sullivan TV guest stint, and her best-selling records, the magazine said of Barbra: "Little girls' dreams and challenges tend to fade in the harsher light of the grown-up world. But this isn't *any* little girl. She's . . . well, she's Barbra Streisand. Anyone else's impossible dream is her reality."

Barbra's next film was announced as Paramount's *On a Clear Day You Can See Forever*, her third musical and the third Streisand vehicle based on a Broadway show. Again, Barbra won the role over its originator (Barbara Harris), but this time there was little talk of miscasting. Barbra seemed perfect for the role of Daisy Gamble, a funky New Yorker with extrasensory perception who makes flowers grow quickly and reveals a prior incarnation as Lady Melinda Winifred Waine-Tentrees, an aristocratic Englishwoman of the nineteenth century.

The role of Dr. Marc Chabot, the hypnotist who discovers Daisy's

With Director Vincente Minnelli on location in New York for On A Clear Day, *1969.*

Canada's Prime Minister Pierre Trudeau escorts Barbra to Winnepeg's Royal Ballet, as romance rumors swirl.

extraordinary powers and past, was to be played by Richard Harris. Af reading the script, however, Harris withdrew, claiming the part was to small. Yves Montand was signed for the role, and filming began in New York. Scenes with Lady Tentrees were filmed in Brighton, England, at one of the country's most opulent structures, the Royal Pavilion. The producers of *On a Clear Day* were the first to receive permission to film in the building, built by George IV as a hunting lodge and now a natior museum.

Permission to film a campus demonstration for the film, however, more difficult to come by. Turned down by Columbia University (wh had been stung shortly before by an actual demonstration) and several other schools, permission was finally obtained from Fordham Universit after Paramount promised to set up two $2,500 scholarships at the scho The demonstration lasts about thirty seconds on the screen.

Barbra's relations with her co-workers on this film were vastly improved. She got along well with her cast and crew, who had heard about—and thus were more tolerant of—Barbra's quest for perfection. S warmed to her director, Vincente Minnelli, whom she had requested because she admired his 1958 film *Gigi*, and her cinematographer, Harr Stradling, whom she had insisted upon after he photographed both *Fur Girl* and *Hello, Dolly!*

Stradling took great care in photographing the famed Streisand visage. "She has youth," he said, "but she's a difficult girl to photograp She knows what's good for her, and 99 percent of her ideas are right." photographing Barbra, Stradling covered his camera lens with a sliding diffusion glass, a trick used to make aging stars look younger. It wasn't Barbra's age which needed hiding, but the scars of youthful acne whic cover her upper cheeks and mar an otherwise beautiful complexion.

On a Clear Day You Can See Forever proved to be a triumph for Streisand. Her personal reviews were the best of her career, with critic praising her comedy timing, her "lightning-like flashes between Melinc airs and Daisy's earthiness" and—to a greater extent than ever before—l beauty. Much mention was made of Barbra's stunning Melinda Tentree especially the scene at the Royal Pavilion in which Melinda, then Lady Moorepark, attempts to arouse Robert Tentrees across a banquet table. toying seductively with a champagne glass. Vincent Canby called it "o of the most graceful Streisand moments ever put on film," and another critic wrote that Harry Stradling's camera "lingers on Barbra's face wi pride—and love." Judith Crist summed up *On a Clear Day* by enthusin: "What a wallow for us Barbra buffs!"

The only sour note to emerge from Barbra's third film was Yves Montand's dissatisfaction with the finished product. "Streisand had the right to cut this film herself," he contended, "so she cut me out so ther could be more of her. Now I just have a supporting role in that film." Judging by the reaction of most critics and audiences to his performan Barbra left too much of Montand in. He was stiff and uncomfortable, and showed as little command of English as he had ten years earlier in his Hollywood debut opposite Marilyn Monroe in *Let's Make Love*. According to one critic, Montand "doesn't destroy the movie singlehandedly—but almost."

Shortly after *On a Clear Day* was completed, Barbra won her seco Golden Globe Award, being named the "World Film Favorite" of 196

After three super-extravagant, elaborately produced musicals with gorgeous costumes and lavish sets, Barbra sought a change of pace. She wanted, she said, to do "a regular little movie—one that doesn't take a whole year to make, cost a zillion dollars and poop you out." The scrip

Comforting Jason on the set of Hell

At a costume party for the Clear Day *cast and crew*

With Herb Ross and George Segal during filming of The Owl and The Pussycat.

she selected was *The Owl and the Pussycat*, a 1964 Broadway success. A two-character play by Bill Manhoff, it had featured Diana Sands, with whom Barbra appeared in *Another Evening with Harry Stoones*, and Alan Alda.

The plot concerned the wild battles and eventual love affair betwe an improbable would-be actress, Doris, who is really a hooker, and a self-styled intellectual and would-be writer, Felix, who is really a bookstore clerk. George Segal was chosen to play Felix.

The Owl and the Pussycat was more of a departure for Barbra tha just being a "regular little movie." It was to be her first non-singing rol and her first totally contemporaneous characterization. Barbra was pleased. "Now, for the first time," she said, "I'm doing without wigs, hairpieces, dyes. It's just going to be me . . . the me that's natural and ve today."

The film's script, written by Buck Henry in his inimitable comedy style, expanded the scope of the play and added several new characters. Henry created wild and hilarious situations shot through with more or "in" sexual jokes.

Being named to his first full directorial assignment was Herbert Ro whose association with Barbra dated back to *I Can Get It For You Wholesale*, for which he staged the musical numbers. He also directed musical numbers for the film version of *Funny Girl*, and had become a close friend of Barbra's. With Ray Stark producing the film, and Harry Stradling photographing her for the fourth straight time, Barbra was among very friendly company.

Was Streisand apprehensive about such a radical change in her film image—from the Fanny Brice-Daisy Gamble innocence to the foul-mouthed lustings of Doris, the part-time prostitute? Hardly. She was described as "delighted" that the film was to be rated X (it was later toned down to get an R) and was pleased to be expanding her range an avoiding stereotype. Perhaps the biggest departure, of course, was the f that *The Owl and the Pussycat* was a non-musical film. Hollywood wondered: Could Streisand handle a straight comedy role? And more importantly, would the public react favorably to a non-singing Barbra? Whatever the risks, she was determined to try.

If Barbra was without apprehension, she wasn't without inhibition. One of her costumes featured two pink hands and a heart sewn over strategic areas, and Barbra was extremely embarrassed when her mothe turned up unexpectedly on the set. "I'm always amazed at the things actresses are made to do," Mrs. Kind said demurely.

The true test of Barbra's new freedom was to be a planned nude scene with George Segal. The script called for Barbra to remove her br and panties, walk across the room to a bed, recline and ask Segal, "Well . . . what do you think?" When the time came for the filming, Barbra froze. Director Ross asked her the trouble. "Herbie," she whispered to him, "I can't. I've got goose bumps and they'll show. Herbie, I just can' What will my mother think?"

Ross, accustomed to coaxing, soothed Barbra's fears, explained the importance of the scene and told her that it would soon all be over. Barbra finally said, "Oh, what the hell, I'll do it once!" Ross describes what happened next: "The set was hushed, the cameras rolled, and Barb threw off her robe and did her first nude scene. It was perfect. I yelled 'Cut and print. Beautiful!' But Barbra is the perfectionist. She wanted a retake. I think we were all shocked, because everybody burst into laughter, including Barbra. We did the retake."

Barbra, however, shouldn't have worried. The finished take lasts o

out five seconds and is very unrevealing, taking place quickly and in
dow. All of Barbra has yet to be seen, and probably won't be. Recently
told an interviewer, "My body is not for public display."

When *The Owl and the Pussycat* was released in November 1970, the
blic responded to Barbra without a song as excitedly as they had to
rbra with. The film was a huge success, primarily due to its outrageously
ny script and the marvelous teamwork of Barbra and George Segal. A
undtrack album was released containing some of the funniest dialogue
d the music of Blood, Sweat and Tears. Although not everyone was
ased, preferring a singing Barbra, the overall reaction was highly
vorable, and *The Owl and the Pussycat* was one of the biggest hits of
70.

After completing four movies in less than three years, Barbra decided
take a vacation from film-making. She devoted herself to Jason, to
corating her apartment, to just relaxing. She told *Life*, "I look forward
working less and simplifying my life, to fulfilling some of my potential
an individual and as a woman. My little-girl fantasy of being a
cording star, a theater star, a concert star and a movie star is impossible
maintain; each of them suffers. There is so much else to learn, so much
re to do. What I'd like is more time—time not only to read the stacks
political journals that have been piling up, but also time to read *Good
ousekeeping* to find out different ways to decorate my son's sand-
ches."

Barbra used her free time not only to read political journals, but to
rticipate actively in political campaigns. She had previously campaigned
r Senator Eugene McCarthy and New York Mayor John Lindsay.
uring 1970 she worked for Congresswoman Bella Abzug, who became a
ose friend. In November, she performed at a "Broadway for Bella"
nefit at Madison Square Garden, made appearances at two fund-raising
rties, and did street campaigning for the Congresswoman.

Barbra also performed at a rally to raise money for members of
ongress who were in the forefront of opposition to the Vietnam War. In
72, she raised money for the Pentagon Papers relief fund by singing
quests over the telephone.

Barbra also used her free time for charitable activities. In 1970, she
as named the Honorary Chairman of the National Association for
tarded Children and has served in that capacity for the last four years.
er movie premieres have been for the benefit of the Police Athletic
ague, The U.N. School and New York's Mayor's Commission on
uth and Physical Fitness, among others. She has performed for the
.N. Children's Fund, The Motion Picture and Television Relief Fund,
he State of Israel Bonds, and SCLF, a Black relief organization.

While Barbra wasn't making movies, the press was reporting one
oject after another being planned for her. It was announced early in
71 that Barbra was scheduled to play Sarah Bernhardt in a Ken Russell
m about the late actress. Anthony Newley announced negotiations for
reisand to star opposite him in a Broadway production about Napoleon
d Josephine. Later, she was reported signed to star in *A Glimpse of
iger*, a film originally started with Kim Darby and Elliot Gould. None
these productions materialized.

Late in 1971, Barbra returned to Las Vegas for a Christmas/New
ear's engagement at the Las Vegas Hilton, formerly the International,
hich she had opened in 1969. The reaction to Barbra's shows at the
ilton was unrestrained joy. Her reviews were among the best of her
reer, and critics praised her as one. The *Las Vegas Visitor* wrote, "The
rformances have reflected Streisand at her greatest. Her tones have

At the Cue *Magazine reception in 1970 at
which she was named "Entertainer of the Year."*

With Ryan O'Neal and Director Peter Bogdanovich on the What's Up, Doc? *set.*

never been more superb, her range more astounding, her personality warmer or more captivating ... The Barbra Streisand holiday performances hold a never-to-be-forgotten experience for those show-goers who demand the ultimate in superlative entertainment."

Barbra soon decided to return to work. During a special screening of Peter Bogdanovich's *The Last Picture Show*, Barbra turned to her escort, John Calley, the head of Warner Brothers, and said, "I want him"—meaning Bogdanovich. Warner Brothers dutifully contacted the director and asked him to step into *A Glimpse of Tiger*. But after he read the script, he balked. "It was kind of a comedy-drama with a lot of social overtones," he said, "and I didn't like it at all. But I said, 'I'd love to work with Barbra. It'll be fun.' And they said, 'Well, what do you have in mind?' And I said, 'Well, I'd like to do kind of a screwball comedy.' " Bogdanovich explained his desire to work with Streisand: "Barbra strikes me as the first person we've had on the screen who's a little bit like Carole Lombard ..." And that is how *What's Up, Doc?* was born.

The script came from an idea of Bogdanovich's (inspired by the 1938 Cary Grant-Katharine Hepburn comedy *Bringing Up Baby*), about a kooky college girl who pursues an absent-minded musicologist and creates incredible havoc. Bogdanovich hired David Newman and Robert Benton, of *Bonnie and Clyde* fame, to write the story. When problems arose, he brought in Buck Henry, and the result was fast, funny slapstick.

Ryan O'Neal, who had been hired to replace Elliot Gould in the ill-fated *A Glimpse of Tiger*, agreed to stay on and co-star in *Doc?*, and after a supporting cast was assembled, production began in San Francisco.

Immediately the Hollywood gossip pens began going furiously: Barbra and Ryan O'Neal were getting along *very* well. Weren't the superstar and the attractive young leading man having a romance? This time the relationship was easily certifiable. Barbra and Ryan were seen everywhere together, attending premieres, going to parties, walking with their children. Soon, newspapers were carrying pictures of the couple on their news pages, with headlines like "A New Love Story?," a reference to the 1970 movie that made O'Neal a star. Not long afterward, he and his wife, Leigh Taylor-Young, separated, adding fuel to the gossipy fires.

The friendship lasted throughout the filming of *What's Up, Doc?* and was played to the hilt by the press and fan magazines. But once the filming was over, Barbra and Ryan went their separate ways. Barbra then began dating Peter Bogdanovich occasionally.

Advance word leaked out that Bogdanovich had a sure hit, and during the first week of March 1972, the following "teaser" ad was placed in New York newspapers: "The boy from *Love Story* meets the girl from *Funny Girl* in a screwball comedy from the director of *The Last Picture Show*." The ad was for a sneak preview planned two days before the film's opening at Radio City Music Hall. Bogdanovich had decided that his film had to be seen with a full audience, who would react to its wild slapstick, to be fully appreciated. He therefore held no special screening for reviewers, who were asked to attend the sneak preview along with the public.

The gambit turned into a near fiasco. Without special passes or a specific section of the theater reserved, the critics had to fend for themselves, and several were unable to get seats until after the film had started. Many were greatly offended by what they considered a slight, and several lukewarm reviews were blamed partially on their pique. As for the audience reaction helping the film, one critic dismissed the viewers that night as "a group of easy laughers."

Despite this inauspicious debut, *What's Up, Doc?* received generally

od reviews and proved to be a smash success at the box office. The
m's characters all meshed wonderfully, and Barbra gave a beautifully
mic performance as Judy Maxwell, as well as singing two songs. The
m was such a financial blockbuster, in fact, that it propelled Barbra to
Box Office magazine designation as "Box Office Champ of the Year"
r 1972, the first time she had achieved that distinction.

Shortly after the completion of What's Up, Doc?, Barbra began
ming Up the Sandbox. The screenplay was by Paul Zindel (author of
e Effect of Gamma Rays on Man-in-the-Moon Marigolds) based on
n Richardson Roiphe's best-selling novel. The story concerns a Man-
ttan housewife who fantasizes herself in various unusual situations to
ieve the boredom of everyday life.

This film was the first Streisand movie produced by her own com-
ny, First Artists, Inc., which she had formed with Paul Newman and
dney Poitier in 1969. Later, Steve McQueen and Dustin Hoffman joined
e group. Commenting about the reason for having her own company,
rbra said, "I have always had to be free to play the roles and sing the
ngs I felt strongly and instinctively were right for me." About her
rtners she added, "I know that my new associates have the same desire
r artistic individuality and total commitment. This company will fill
at need for each individual and at the same time we'll have a teamwork
uation based on mutual respect and understanding."

In Up the Sandbox Barbra's character, Margaret Reynolds, was the
ost dominant central figure of any movie she had yet made. The rela-
vely small role of her husband, Paul, was to be played by David Selby,
ho was a regular on daytime TV's Dark Shadows for two and a half
ars. Irvin Kershner was set to direct.

After location shooting in Manhattan, at the Statue of Liberty and on
ong Island, the production company flew to Kenya to film a scene in
hich Margaret fantasizes herself in Africa to learn the Somburu Tribe's
cret of painless childbirth. Barbra arrived in Sanburo, 200 miles north of
airobi, with eighteen pieces of luggage, a secretary, two friends, Jason
d a bag of chicken bones. The bones were for the benefit of Jason, who
as planning to do some archaeological exploration; Barbra brought them
st in case his efforts failed to turn up any actual prehistoric relics. Later,
son made his screen debut as an extra in this film. The Somburu tribes-
ople were alternately amazed and frightened by the elaborate pro-
ction equipment. Barbra, who hates to be photographed, wandered
ound taking pictures of the local citizens incessantly. At one point she
ked a native girl to apply some of her blue eye make-up to Barbra's
elids. As Barbra tells it, "She broke a twig from a tree, took a long
read from her husband's skirt, made like a Q-tip, broke off a piece of
ft blue rock, spit on it, and put that on my eye with the Q-tip. Now I
t all my eye shadow on with a Q-tip."

Up the Sandbox was scheduled to open during Christmas week, 1972,
New York City. First Artists, Inc., had two other films opening at the
me time, The Getaway, with Steve McQueen and Ali MacGraw, and
he Life and Times of Judge Roy Bean, with Paul Newman. Prior to the
emiere, Barbra, usually reticent about meeting the press, began giving
terviews. She explained her new openness to Earl Wilson: "I care about
ndbox. I think it is a provocative film and I want to help it."

She told another interviewer, The New York Times' Guy Flatley,
at Margaret Reynolds and Barbra Streisand have a great deal in
mmon. "There is a part of me that longs to stay home and be with my
ild ... but there is another part of me that needs a form of expression
her than bearing children, just as there is another part of Margaret that

*With Paul Newman and Sidney Poitier as they
announce the formation of their company, First
Artists, Inc. in 1969.*

Modelling the lace dress she designed for her 1971 Christmas engagement at the Las Vegas Hilton.

With Director Irvin Kershner on location in New York for Up The Sandbox.

feels love is not enough." Discussing Margaret's fantasies, Barbra said, "Fantasies can make a rich inner life. They can lead you places. If I never had a fantasy about being an actress, perhaps I wouldn't have become one."

These weren't the only similarities between Barbra and her character. "The family in the movie is partly based on my family," Barbra told Flatley. "That scene at the door—when Margaret tells her mother she doesn't want to see her today—I've played that scene with my own mother several times."

When *Up the Sandbox* opened at the Coronet and Loew's State II Theatres in New York on December 21, 1972, it met with a decidedly mixed reaction; the critical response, in fact, was as widely varied as any in film history. It ranged from *The New York Times* calling the film "a joy" and *Cue* magazine terming it "funny, exhilarating and mature" to the *New York Daily News* pegging it as "a confusing comedy" and *Variety* totally dismissing it as "an untidy melange of overproduced, heavy-handed fantasy. . . ."

Barbra's personal notices, however, were more uniform. As usual, they were excellent. Judith Crist of *New York* magazine said, "Barbra Streisand gives the finest performance of her career," and Pauline Kael of *The New Yorker* opined, "Barbra Streisand is a complete reason for going to a movie, as Garbo was."

The film was a financial disappointment, especially after the huge success of *What's Up, Doc?*, but it is an effort of which Barbra may be justly proud. Representing a giant step forward in her career, it is the first movie in which she portrays a relatively average human being. No longer, in this film, was she Barbra Streisand, superstar, but rather she became Margaret Reynolds, creating a real, sympathetic character about whom we could not help but care. It is a characterization worthy of a truly fine actress.

Another fine Streisand characterization came out of Barbra's seventh film, *The Way We Were*. Based on Arthur Laurents' novel, it is the story of Katie Morosky, a campus radical in the late 1930s, and her improbable romance with Hubbell Gardiner, a carefree college jock, played by Robert Redford. Produced by Ray Stark and directed by Sydney Pollack, the movie began filming in late 1972.

Location shooting took place in upstate New York, Manhattan and Southern California. Union College in Schenectady, New York, was the site for the campus sequences. The ivy-covered buildings of the college were perfect for an evocation of the era, and Pollack took care not to film any of the new, modern structures dotting the area. Making the students look like scholars of the late 1930s was a bit more difficult. About 750 students at Union were used as extras, and studio hairdressers worked assembly-line style to trim the boys' long hair, beards and moustaches. Most of the students were more than willing to shed their locks for a chance to appear in the movie.

Filming then moved to Manhattan, where things proceeded smoothly. Barbra's reputation for friendships with her leading men followed her, however, and one of the film's extras reports that Mrs. Redford, after visiting the set with two of her children, instructed them to remain and "keep an eye on Daddy." Nothing ever developed between the two stars, although Redford is full of praise for Streisand. "I liked her," he says, "and we got along very well. I found her very talented, intelligent, insecure and untrusting. Untrusting because she's been told too many lies, she's been hustled, misled, used and jounced by too many hangers-on and hucksters."

he film's final scenes were shot in California. During one, a costume
at which everyone had to come as a Marx Brother, Groucho paid a
se visit to the set and exchanged fast Marxisms with cast and crew.
he Way We Were gives us Barbra in the fashion look of the '30s
the style is very becoming. The sets are marvelously evocative of
a, and the film is a nostalgic love story like those that very same era
ced. The teaming of Streisand and Redford creates electricity on
reen, and their performances are superb. In this film, Barbra con-
to fulfill the acting promise evident in *Up the Sandbox*.

While the majority of critics have hailed the stars, the film has been
y criticized, primarily because of its incomplete treatment of the
care of the late 1940s, which, in the film, helps to break up Katie
ubbell's marriage. The subject is never fully explored, and never
ncingly made the catalyst for the break-up. In Laurents' novel, this is
t clearly made—Katie leaves Hubbell because she knows that her
Communist associations will blacklist her husband and ruin his career.
s Katie's supreme sacrifice, and it is entirely consistent with her
cal commitments and her love for Hubbell. In the film, this is never
explained, and their marriage dissolves through sheer incompatibility.
explanation fails because they were *always* incompatible, and they
it.

ronically, a scene describing Katie's sacrifice and several others
ng a point of the horrors of the Blacklist were filmed, and included in
versions of the film. They were dropped after several sneak prev-

Despite the film's flaws, it was one of the biggest hits of 1973, and
nbia claims it is on its way to becoming their biggest grosser ever.
oox-office appeal of Streisand and Redford in a nostalgic love story
ure-fire blockbuster from the outset.

Up the Sandbox and *The Way We Were* bode very well for Barbra's
opment as a dramatic actress. At the close of her first decade, she
ccessfully avoided stereotype, tackling an assortment of roles and
genres. She has progressed from spectacular re-created nostalgia to
ost contemporary of characterizations. More importantly, she has
many of her patented gestures, inflections and accents; she has con-
ated less on re-creating Barbra Streisand and more on creating real
cters.

After her last few performances, it seems more probable that Barbra
someday be able to successfully portray the classical heroines she has
he would like to attempt—Juliet, L'Aiglon, Camille and Medea. It is
now that when Barbra feels herself ready to handle such roles, she
certainly play them credibly. After the accomplishments of Barbra
and's first decade, there are few who could argue with Vincent
y's observation: "Talent such as hers will not break when tested, it
mes enriched."

Barbra and Robert Redford all dressed up for the wedding scene in The Way We Were. *It was cut from the film.*

With Kay Medford

156

FUNNY GIRL

A Columbia Pictures Release of a Rastar Productions
Picture (1968). In Panavision and Technicolor.
Rated G.

CAST

Fanny Brice   Barbra Streisand
Nick Arnstein   Omar Sharif
Rose Brice   Kay Medford
Georgia James   Anne Francis
Florenz Ziegfeld   Walter Pidgeon
Eddie Ryan   Lee Allen
Mrs. Strakosh   Mae Questel
Branca   Gerald Mohr
Keeney   Frank Faylen
Emma   Mittie Lawrence
Mrs. O'Malley   Gertrude Flynn
Mrs. Meeker   Penny Stanton
Company manager   John Harmon
The Ziegfeld girls:
    Thordis Brandt, Bettina Brenna, Virginia
    Ann Ford, Alena Johnston, Karen Lee, Mary
    Jane Mangler, Inga Neilsen, Sharon Vaughn

CREDITS

Produced by   Ray Stark
Directed by   William Wyler
Screenplay by   Isobel Lennart
Based on the play with music by   Jule Styne
Lyrics by   Bob Merrill
Book by   Isobel Lennart from the original story by
    Miss Lennart and produced by   Rastar Productions
Musical numbers directed by   Herbert Ross
Music by   Jule Styne
Lyrics by   Bob Merrill
"My Man" music by   Maurice Yvain
French lyrics by   A. Willemetz and Jacques Charles
English adaptation by   Channing Pollack
"Second Hand Rose" by   James F. Hanley and Grant Clarke
"I'd Rather Be Blue"   by Fred Fisher and Billy Rose
Production designed by   Gene Callahan
Costumes designed by   Irene Sharaff
Photography by   Harry Stradling, A.S.C.
Music supervised and conducted by   Walter Scharf
Unit production manager   Paul Helmick
Set decorator   William Kiernan
Assistant directors   Jack Roe, Ray Gosnell
Assistants to producer   David Dworski, Lorry McCauley
Properties   Richard M. Rubin
Script supervisor   Marshall Schlom
Furs by   Reiss & Fabrizio
Make-up supervision   Ben Lane
Make-up artist   Frank McCoy
Hairstyles by   Vivienne Walker, Virginia Darcy
Vocal-dance arrangements   Betty Walberg
Music editor   Ted Sebern
Public relations   Jack Brodsky
Art director   Robert Luthardt
Supervising film editor   Robert Swink
Film editors   Maury Winetrobe, William Sands
Sound supervisor   Charles J. Rice
Sound   Arthur Piantadosi, Jack Solomon
Orchestration by   Jack Hayes, Walter Scharf, Leo Shuken,
        Herbert Spencer

"I'm The Greatest Star"(with Lee Allen)

SYNOPSIS

At the New Amsterdam Theater, Ziegfeld Follies star Fanny Brice (Barbra Streisand) recalls the ups and downs of her rise to stardom. She remembers her mother's friends telling her to forget show business ("If a Girl Isn't Pretty") because, among other things, "if a girl's incidentals are no bigger than two lentils, then to me it doesn't spell success."

Undaunted, she tries out for a job at Keeney's Music Hall, where she is hired by sympathetic Eddie Ryan (Lee Allen) and quickly fired by Mr. Keeney (Frank Faylen) because she has "skinny legs." She tries to convince Keeney of her talent ("I'm the Greatest Star") but he remains unmoved. Eddie decides to put Fanny in a musical number planned for the next night, after getting her promise that she can roller skate.

She can't, and the number ("The Roller Skate Rag") is hilariously disrupted by Fanny's ineptitude. The audience loves it, and Fanny stays on to sing "I'd Rather Be Blue." Her combination of shyness, coyness and a beautiful voice endears her to the audience and convinces Keeney to hire her.

Backstage to express his appreciation of her performance is Nick Arnstein (Omar Sharif), a dashing figure with a ruffled shirt whom Fanny finds "gorgeous." He invites her to dinner, but she declines, since she is expected at a party at her mother's saloon. As Nick leaves, Fanny resigns herself to never seeing him again.

Fanny stars at Keeney's for six months until Florenz Ziegfeld (Walter Pidgeon) asks her to audition for his new Follies. Her rendition of "Second Hand Rose" charms Ziegfeld, and he puts her into the finale of the show, a sumptuous bridal number ("His Love Makes Me Beautiful"). Fanny objects, explaining that if she sings those words, the audience will laugh at her. Ziegfeld disagrees, and tells her that she either sings the song as written, or leaves the Follies. When the number is presented, Fanny plays it for laughs: she appears hugely pregnant as she sings, "I am the beautiful reflection of my love's affection . . ."

Ziegfeld is furious, but the audience gives Fanny five curtain calls and he grudgingly acknowledges her comic success. Backstage once again is Nick Arnstein, who has sent her flowers and again invites her out to dinner. She must decline once more, however, because her mother is throwing a block party in her honor. She asks Arnstein if he would like to attend, and to her surprise he accepts. After the party, Fanny and Nick reveal their mutual need for meaningful companionship ("People"). But Nick, a professional gambler, must leave for Kentucky, where he has just bought a race horse. It is not until more than a year later that they meet again, in Baltimore.

This time, Fanny goes to dinner and Nick proceeds to express his desire for her ("You Are Woman, I Am Man"). They spend several days together in Baltimore, but when it is time for the Follies to move on to Chicago, Nick must catch a boat to Europe in order to play cards and recoup losses suffered in a horserace earlier that day. When Nick tells Fanny he loves her, she resolves to follow him to Europe, against the advice of her fellow Follies stars ("Don't Rain on My Parade").

After Nick wins enough money to get back on his feet, he and Fanny are married. They move into a mansion on Long Island ("Sadie, Sadie") and soon there is "a beautiful reflection of my love's affection," a daughter, Frances.

"His Love Makes Me Beautiful"

With Omar Sharif

The marriage is idyllic until Nick fails in an attempt to strike oil. He loses the house and the Arnsteins move into an apartment in Manhattan. Hoping to break his unlucky streak, Nick gets involved in a card game, missing Fanny's newest opening night performance ("The Swan"). Fanny is worried, then hurt and angry when he fails to appear. He tells her that his chance to change his luck was more important to him than her opening night. His luck hadn't changed, however, and he is deeper in debt than ever.

Distraught when her mother (Kay Medford) tells her the depths of Nick's financial troubles, Fanny secretly puts up money to make Nick a partner in a new gambling casino. When he finds out what she has done, he is incensed that he has become so dependent upon his wife. In an attempt to salvage some of his pride, he accepts an offer to join in on a phony bond deal. Before long, he is arrested for embezzlement.

Pleading guilty to the charge, Nick is sentenced to 18 months in prison. He tells Fanny to divorce him, because he is tired of trying to keep up with her success. Fanny asks him to wait until his release and, if he still feels the same way then, "I won't fight you."

The film's closing scene returns us to the opening, with Fanny waiting for Nick's return. When he arrives, he tells her that he has not changed his mind. She is heartbroken, but resolves to go on with her life and not let her sorrow overcome her. Her performance that night becomes her rallying point as she sings "My Man."

With Lee Allen and Omar Sharif

"You Are Woman, I Am Man"

With Omar Sharif

With Lee Allen

As Baby Snooks

"Ray Stark's *Funny Girl* is just what was anticipated: [r]unning musical production in the Florenz Ziegfeld tra-[diti]on encompassing the tender, tragic love story of the [uns]urpassed Fanny Brice and her professional gambler [hus]band, Nick Arnstein. . . . Miss Streisand, vastly talented, [giv]es a glowing performance in her portrayal of the most [nota]ble comedienne of her time. The actress is comical in [the] sketches, her voice is clear and pure, she is wistful in [love], deliriously happy in the early part of her marriage [a]nd reduced to tears when the marriage falls apart . . . [Str]eisand's last number, 'My Man,' at the finale is so beau-[tifu]lly staged and sung, the audience was stunned for a [mo]ment and then burst into wild applause."

WANDA HALE,
New York Daily News

"Let me preface my remarks about *Funny Girl* with a [stat]ement or three about Barbra Streisand. I have followed [her] meteoric career . . . being enthralled by her intense [sing]ing style on stage, in numerous recordings and a few [tele]vision spectaculars. Simply, I love Barbra. But I did not [love] the film *Funny Girl*. I enjoyed the earlier sequences, [but] as I watched the film go to pieces and crumble around [Mis]s Streisand's shapely legs in the second half, I felt sorry [for] both for Miss Streisand and for the audience. We were [bot]h being cheated. We are presented with an overblown, [na]useatingly fake Hollywood production. Henry Street [loo]ks like a typical Hollywood sound set, spanking clean [and] oh! so charming. There are herring stands, and push [car]ts, and delicate immigrants struggling with English and [bei]ng impressed by telegrams. Somewhere in Hollywood [the]re must be real garbage. "A bit of paté . . . I drink it all [up]" sums up the cutesy ethnic humor. Mr. Wyler has [acc]epted Miss Lennart's phony and more typische-than-[typ]ische concept of the Yiddish idiom."

DONALD J. MAYERSON,
The Villager

"At one point in the movie *Funny Girl*, Nick Arn-[stei]n reads a newspaper review of his wife's performance [in] the Ziegfeld Follies: '. . . All a show needs is Fanny [Bri]ce,' he says. Perhaps the best way to describe the big, [sch]maltzy movie . . . and its star, is to say: All a show [nee]ds is Barbra Streisand. The Brooklyn born talent [dan]ces, sings, jokes and beautifully acts her way through [the] nearly three-hour film. . . . She comes across on the [scr]een as a fragile beauty, with cameras picking up details [and] closeups which give the audience a much more inti-[ma]te knowledge of one of the world's most loved comedi-[enn]es, Miss Fanny Brice. Barbra's performance is flawless. [It] is a movie full of old-fashioned emotions, fun, music [and] entertainment fit for anyone old enough to remember [Mis]s Brice or young enough to be enchanted by Miss [Str]eisand."

BARBARA SPECTOR,
Newark Evening News

"No more cracks about Barbra Streisand's nose. After *Funny Girl*, they'll be as obsolete as Harold Teen Comics. It took the combined efforts of God knows how many people to do it, but I'll be damned if they haven't made her beautiful. In the most remarkable screen debut I will probably ever see in my lifetime, the toadstool from Eras-mus High School has been turned into a truffle, and I, for one, couldn't be happier about the transformation . . . When Streisand is around, she turns *Funny Girl* from dis-guised Technicolor wide-screen hokum into something bordering on art. With her voice, with her walk, with her emotion, and with the passion of her hydroelectric power, she makes tickets something worth buying. Everyone else should have stayed in bed."

REX REED

"The script is just a vehicle for showing off one of the most exciting musical comedy stars in a decade. Miss Streisand, who has already conquered stage, television and the record business, is now an all-media star. Barbra Strei-sand's triumphant movie debut in *Funny Girl* is certain to get her an Academy Award nomination.

" 'I'm a bagel on a plateful of onion rolls,' she explains. Or, she wonders petulantly, 'You think beautiful girls are going to stay in style forever?' She says that her marriage ceremony upset her because the groom was prettier than the bride. During most of the film, she cuts through the potential sentimentality with self-mocking humor that makes the world laugh with her rather than at her. This was Fanny Brice's technique for survival, and Barbra Streisand also understands it and uses it superlatively."

JOSEPH GELMIS,
Newsday

"Streisand has the gift of making old written dialogue sound like inspired improvisation; almost every line she says seems to have just sprung to mind and out. Her inflections are witty and surprising, and, more surpris-ingly, delicate; she can probably do more for a line than any screen comedienne since Jean Arthur, in the thirties . . . It is Streisand's peculiar triumph that in the second half, when the routine heartbreak comes, as it apparently must in all musical biographies, she shows an aptitude for suffering that those (other) actresses didn't. Where they became sanctimonious and noble, thereby violating every-thing we had loved them for, she simply drips as unself-consciously and impulsively as a true tragic muse. And the tears belong to her face; they seem to complete it, as Garbo's suffering in *Camille* seemed to complete her beauty."

PAULINE KAEL,
The New Yorker

NOTES

Barbra's first movie was a brilliant debut which made her an instant Hollywood superstar and won her the Academy Award as Best Actress of 1968. The film was nominated as Best Picture. Early in her career, Barbra had commented that when she was young, "being a star meant being a *movie* star." With *Funny Girl*, Barbra was undoubtedly a *star*.

HELLO, DOLLY!

A 20th Century-Fox Release of a Chenault Productions, Inc. Picture (1969). In Todd-AO and Magna Color by Deluxe. Rated G.

CAST

Dolly Levi	Barbra Streisand
Horace Vandergelder	Walter Matthau
Cornelius Hackl	Michael Crawford
Orchestra leader	Louis Armstrong
Irene Malloy	Marianne McAndrew
Minnie Fay	E. J. Peaker
Barnaby Tucker	Danny Lockin
Ermengarde	Joyce Ames
Ambrose Kemper	Tommy Tune
Gussie Granger	Judy Knaiz
Rudolph Reisenweber	David Hurst
Fritz	Fritz Feld
Vandergelder's barber	Richard Collier
Policeman in park	J. Pat O'Malley

CREDITS

Produced by	Ernest Lehman
Screenplay by	Ernest Lehman
Directed by	Gene Kelly
Associate producer	Roger Edens
Dance and musical numbers staged by	Michael Kidd
Music and lyrics by	Jerry Herman
Music scored and conducted by	Lennie Hayton
	Lionel Newman
Photography by	Harry Stradling, A.S.C.
Production designed by	John De Cuir
Art direction	Jack Martin Smith
	Herman Blumenthal
Costumes designed by	Irene Sharaff
Set decorations by	Walter M. Scott
	George Hopkins
	Raphael Bretton
Edited by	William Reynolds, A.C.E.
Unit production manager	Francisco Day
Assistant director	Paul Helmick
Sound supervision	James Corcoran
Sound	Murray Spivak, Vinton Vernon,
	Jack Solomon, Douglas Williams
Assistant choreographer	Shelah Hackett
Orchestrations	Philip Lang, Lennie Hayton,
	Joseph Lipman, Don Costa,
	Alexander Courage, Warren Barker
	Frank Comstock, Herbert Spencer
Dance arrangements	Marvin Laird
Choral arrangements	Jack Latimer
Music editors	Robert Mayer, Kenneth Wannberg
Special photographic effects	
	L. B. Abbott, A.S.C., Art Cruickshank
Make-up supervision	Dan Striepeke
Make-up artists	Ed Butterworth, Richard Hamilton
Hairstyling by	Edith Lindon
Wardrobe	Ed Wynigear, Barbara Westerland
Public relations	Patricia Newcomb
Script supervisor	Mollie Kent
Dialogue coach	George Eckert
Based on the stage play produced by	David Merrick
Book of stage play by	Michael Stewart
Based on "The Matchmaker" by	Thornton Wilder
Music and lyrics of stage play by	Jerry Herman
Directed and choreographed by	Gower Champion

SYNOPSIS

Mrs. Dolly Levi (Barbra Streisand), a well-known young widow and matchmaker, has agreed to find a mate for Horace Vandergelder (Walter Matthau), a successful merchant in Yonkers, New York ("Just Leave Everything to Me"). Horace has his eye on Irene Malloy (Marianne McAndrew), who owns a millinery shop in Manhattan. He informs his two timid and overworked clerks, Cornelius (Michael Crawford) and Barnaby (Danny Lockin) of his need for a wife ("It Takes a Woman"). When Dolly meets Horace, she decides that she wants him for herself ("It Takes a Woman—Reprise"). When Horace announces he is going to propose to Irene, Dolly goes into action to prevent this.

In the meantime, Horace has denied permission for his niece Ermengarde (Joyce Ames) to marry Ambrose (Tommy Tune), a penniless painter. Dolly overhears Ambrose suggesting they elope, and she tells them she'll arrange everything: she'll take Ermengarde to Manhattan as she promised Horace, who wants her to forget Ambrose. But Ambrose is to come to New York as well, explains Dolly, and the two young people will enter a polka contest at the Harmonia Gardens, where Dolly used to go frequently with her late husband and is well known. They will win the polka contest, Dolly goes on, and will use the prize money to get married. She asks them to tell the head waiter at the Harmonia Gardens, "Dolly's coming back!"

Dolly then discovers that Barnaby and Cornelius are plotting to close the shop and go to New York, but they bemoan the fact that they know no girls there. Dolly gives them the address of Irene's hat shop, and tells them to be there at 2:00, but not to say who sent them. Excited by their impending trips to Manhattan, everyone converges on the train station ("Put on Your Sunday Clothes").

In New York City, Irene complains about her lack of romance ("Ribbons Down My Back"). When Cornelius and Barnaby arrive, she flirts with them, but is amazed when Barnaby dives under a table and Cornelius into a cupboard upon the arrival of Horace and Dolly. Before Horace can propose to Irene, he senses the presence of people hiding, but he doesn't know who they are. When Irene refuses to explain, Horace leaves in a huff, much to Dolly's delight. She suggests that the boys take Irene and her assistant Minnie Fay (E.J. Peaker) to the Harmonia Gardens for dinner. The boys have no money, but decide to fake it. When Cornelius says he can't dance, Dolly teaches him ("Dancing").

Alone now, Dolly begins to miss her late husband. She speaks aloud to him, saying she intends to find happiness again before it is too late ("Before the Parade Passes By").

Irene and Minnie meet the boys for dinner. Since they haven't enough money for carfare, they convince the girls that walking is the elegant thing to do ("Elegance"). At the same time, in her dressing room, Dolly muses that life with Horace will not be the same as life with her husband, Ephraim. But she convinces herself that she shouldn't expect it to be ("Love Is Only Love").

At the Harmonia Gardens, the waiters are waiting for Dolly's impending return. She enters atop a great ornate stairway and greets her old friends, who return the affection in kind ("Hello, Dolly!"). She is soon joined by the Gardens' orchestra leader (Louis Armstrong) and her return is a triumph. Later, she broaches the subject of marriage to Horace, but before he can react he spies

With Danny Lockin, Michael Crawford, Marianne McAndrew and E.J. Peaker

With Walter Matthau

Relaxing on the set

"Dancing" (with Michael Crawford)

With Michael Crawford and Marianne McAndrew

"Before the Parade Passes By" (with Walter Matthau)

Ermengarde dancing with Ambrose, and charges on to the floor in a rage. He then sees Barnaby and Cornelius, and fires them on the spot. His anger causes a great disturbance, which disrupts the entire Harmonia Gardens.

Outside, Cornelius tells Irene that he loves her, even though they've just met. ("It Only Takes a Moment"). Dolly, walking away from the disgruntled Horace, tells him he'll be sorry in a stinging goodbye ("So Long Dearie"). The next morning Horace realizes that he needs Dolly. He blesses the engagement of his niece to Ambrose, makes Cornelius his partner and promotes Barnaby, and proposes to Dolly. They are wed ("Finale") and Dolly promises she'll "never go away again."

169

"Hello, Dolly!" (with Louis Armstrong)

With Walter Matthau

"So Long Dearie" (with Walter Matthau)

"*Hello, Dolly!* is an expensive, expansive, sometimes exaggerated, G-rated, wholesome, pictorially opulent musical which rides in on the David Merrick stage and Hit Parade momentum and with the charisma of Barbra Streisand in the title role. A truly pre-sold title, the pic looks on screen the $20 million it stands on the books. It is a warm-hearted and splashy extravaganza, harmlessly hyperbolic and a good gamble to pay on the risks taken. At a guess some may complain that Miss Streisand's title role, younger than the others and possibly more on the cool side, subtracts something of compassion. It is still a dolly of a Dolly on its own terms and she is, after the property itself, the big selling value."

Variety

"In *Hello, Dolly!*, Streisand has almost nothing to work with. It's a star role, of course—a role that seems to release something triumphant in an actress—but the songs are dismal affairs, with lyrics that make one's teeth ache, and the smirky dialogue might pass for wit among not too bright children. . . . The movie is full of that fake, mechanical exhilaration of big Broadway shows—the gut-busting, muscle-straining dance that is meant to wow you. This dancing, like the choral singing, is asexual and unromantic, and goes against the little farce plot about the matching up of several pairs of lovers. At the center of all this asexuality, impersonality, and noisy mediocrity, there Streisand, an actress who uses song as an intensification of emotion. She's not like the singers who are sometimes passable actresses if you don't push them beyond a small range. She opens up such abundance of emotion that it dissolves the coarseness of the role. There's no telling what she *can't* do. Almost unbelievably, she turns this star role back into a woman, so that the show seems to be about something."

PAULINE KAEL,
The New Yorker

"There she stands at the head of the great ornate stairway, her glorious merry-widow figure draped in a ton of jeweled gold, a spray of feathers in her belle epoque topknot. She is smiling her sly, secret, Brooklyn-Jewish-girl-who-made-it-big smile. The film is at its climax, she is the champion female movie star of her time and she is poised for the most played, the most familiar, the most parodied song of the decade. We are expectant. Will she bring it off? Will she top all the toppers? Boys, the kid's a winner. The whole thing's a triumph. She was smiling that sly smile because she knew all the time she was going to kill us."

RICHARD COHEN,
Women's Wear Daily

"Miss Streisand's obvious youth and real sexuality obliterated any sense of nostalgia in the *Hello, Dolly!* number and add a curious ambiguity to other aspects of the role, including her speeches directed to Mr. Levi, her late husband. (I had the odd feeling that she must have been married to him at eight and lost him at ten.) The star, a fine if limited comedienne, impersonates Dolly as a teen-age Mae West, circling around the role and finding laughs occasionally, but never quite committing herself to it."

VINCENT CANBY,
The New York Times

"To immortalize the role of Dolly Levi, a damned exasperating woman and matchmaker, on celluloid, Barbra Streisand was chosen. The decision was economically sound, but artistically unwise. Miss Streisand is too real and honest a performer to carry off a cartoon character like Mrs. Levi. The part calls for a touch of madness and Miss Streisand is too sane."

DONALD J. MAYERSON,
The Villager

"In *Dolly*, Miss Streisand is required to play someone other than herself, and she can't. She gives instead her night club act. Her songs are delivered with all those mannerisms of dropping eyes, fluttering hands and snaking fingers that endear her to camp followers. . . . When she sings, the songs get the standard Streisand treatment. The refrain is sung the first time in a funereal beat with the words released as if they were stretched over an elastic band."

BRUCE BAHRENBURG,
Newark Evening News

"Barbra Streisand, the umpteenth *Dolly*, is magnificent as always in a role that apparently brings out the best in those who attempt it. And the best of Barbra Streisand has got to be the best there is. As the con woman of Yonkers, circa 1890, she can get you what you want when you want it, and can make you need what she has when she has it. . . . As a legitimate, straight singer, she is without peer, her loud, clear and strikingly identifiable voice of inestimable benefit to whatever she chooses to sing. But more than that she is a complete performer. Her comedic talents are exceptional, her comprehension of material perfect. When she is on screen, *Hello, Dolly!* bubbles over, but all too often, especially during the first half of the film, she is missing. Such is her talent that she can carry any kind of material—much more burdening stuff than this marshmallow—but she has to be given the chance."

JOE ROSEN,
New York Morning Telegraph

NOTE

Hello, Dolly! was nominated for an Academy Award as the Best Picture of 1969. It won three technical Oscars.

With Laurie Main

With Yves Montand

ON A CLEAR DAY
YOU CAN SEE FOREVER

A Paramount Picture (1970). In Panavision and Technicolor. Rated G.

CAST

Daisy Gamble	Barbra Streisand
Dr. Marc Chabot	Yves Montand
Dr. Mason Hume	Bob Newhart
Warren Pratt	Larry Blyden
Dr. Conrad Fuller	Simon Oakland
Tad Pringle	Jack Nicholson
Robert Tentrees	John Richardson
Mrs. Fitzherbert	Pamela Brown
Winnie Wainwhisle	Irene Handl
Prince Regent	Roy Kinnear
Divorce attorney	Peter Crowcroft
Prosecuting attorney	Byron Webster
Mrs. Hatch	Mabel Albertson
Lord Percy	Laurie Main
Hoyt III	Kermit Murdock
Muriel	Elaine Giftos
Diana Smallwood	Angela Pringle
Clews	Leon Ames
Millard	Paul Camen
Wytelipt	George Neise
Preston	Tony Colti

CREDITS

Produced by	Howard W. Koch
Directed by	Vincente Minnelli
Screenplay by	Alan Jay Lerner
Music by	Burton Lane
Lyrics by	Alan Jay Lerner
Based on the musical play	
	"On a Clear Day You Can See Forever"
Director of photography	Harry Stradling, A.S.C.
Production design by	John De Cuir
Unit production managers	Sergi Petschnikoff
	Howard Roessel
Assistant director	William McGarry
Edited by	David Bretherton, A.C.E.
Set decoration	George Hopkins
	Ralph Bretton
Contemporary costumes by	Arnold Scaasi
Period costumes by	Cecil Beaton
Music supervised, arranged and conducted by	
	Nelson Riddle
Script continuity	Molly Kent Wade
Dialogue coach	Walter Kelley
Hairstyles by	Frederick Glaser
Time lapse photography by	John Ott
Choreography	Howard Jeffrey
Vocal-dance arrangements by	Betty Walberg
Make-up supervision	Harry Ray
Sound recording	Benjamin Winkler
	Elden Ruberg
Aerial photography by	Tyler Camera Systems
Titles by	Wayne Fitzgerald
Choral arrangements	Joseph J. Lilley
Wardrobe	John Anderson
	Shirlee Strahm

Co-starring
Bob Newhart / Larry Blyden / Simon Oakland / Jack Nicholson and John Richardson
Music by Burton Lane   Screenplay and Lyrics by Alan Jay Lerner   Produced by Howard W. Koch
Directed by Vincente Minnelli   Music Arranged and Conducted by Nelson Riddle
Panavision® Technicolor® A Paramount Picture "G"—All Ages Admitted General Audiences
Sound track album available on Columbia Records

SYNOPSIS

Daisy Gamble (Barbra Streisand) is a young New Yorker who makes flowers grow—fast ("Hurry! It's Lovely up Here!"). She can also tell when the phone is about to ring, and she knows where lost items can be located. These powers, however, are not what's troubling her. Instead, she wants to quit smoking so that she can live up to the standards set by Chemical Foods, Inc., for employees' wives, since her fiancé, Warren (Larry Blyden), is about to be hired by the company.

She goes to Dr. Marc Chabot (Yves Montand), a hypnotist at Stuyvesant University, to be cured of her addiction. While under hypnosis, Daisy begins to speak in a strange voice and reveals a previous incarnation as Melinda Winifred Waine-Tentrees, an aristocratic Englishwoman of the nineteenth century. In response to Dr. Chabot's incredulous questions, Melinda tells him of her early life in the Angel of Mercy Orphanage and her marriage to Lord Percy Moorepark (Laurie Main), whom she describes as one of the richest and most boring men in England. Melinda describes a dinner at which she meets Robert Tentrees (John Richardson), a handsome, dashing and shiftless aristocrat whom she toasts in her most seductive manner across the banquet table ("Love With All the Trimmings"). They begin an affair, which they make sure Lord Percy discovers. He divorces Melinda, and she and Robert are wed.

At each session to cure Daisy of her smoking, she reveals more and more details of Melinda's life. Dr. Chabot is intrigued, but believes that all of it has some basis in Daisy's current life and that she is subconsciously making it all up. He reports the details of the case to his students, without revealing the subject, and is sure the mystery will soon be solved. At future sessions, however, Chabot finds himself falling in love with Melinda. It is this seemingly irrational reaction which first makes him realize that Melinda must truly have existed ("Melinda").

Daisy, meanwhile, has become attracted to Dr. Chabot. At home, she can't sleep trying to decide between the man she is attracted to and the one she is committed to ("Go to Sleep"). This isn't counting her ex-stepbrother, Tad (Jack Nicholson), who wants Daisy for himself.

Word has leaked out about Dr. Chabot's strange case and the press makes the story as sensational as possible. Students begin to demonstrate in favor of Dr. Chabot's research. Worried, the University demands that Chabot deny any "mystical implications" in the case. Daisy comes to the doctor's apartment to inquire how well he is holding up under the strain of publicity and to ask who "the nut" is. He doesn't tell her; instead he hypnotizes her by telepathy and speaks to Melinda. She sorrowfully tells him that Robert Tentrees has deserted her and, although he was her husband, he never understood her as well as Dr. Chabot ("He Isn't You").

The University takes back its demand that Dr. Chabot deny the possibility of reincarnation when it learns that its chief benefactor wants to learn as much as possible about the subject, so that he can discover who he'll be in the future and leave all his money to himself. Unfortunately, things go awry when Daisy accidentally plays a tape recording of her sessions with Dr. Chabot. She realizes that she is "the nut," and she learns that not only does Dr.

With John Richardson and Laurie Main

Chabot think nothing of her, but he loves Melinda, her former self ("What Did I Have That I Don't Have?"). Daisy is furious and tells Dr. Chabot to leave her alone.

The doctor insists that Daisy is valuable for scientific research and he tries to phone her. Since she knows it is him when he calls, she never answers. When he comes to her apartment, she orders him out, telling him to "stop using my head for a motel" for his meetings with Melinda. Desperate, Chabot decides to speak to Daisy by telepathy and she then hears his voice constantly ("Come Back to Me"). Finally, she goes to his office. He tells her that not only is she not "a nut," but she might be the most totally sane person ever. He tells her that she must glory in her powers, not hide them. ("On a Clear Day"—Montand). She agrees to one final session, during which she reveals fourteen previous incarnations and several future ones —including one in which she and Dr. Chabot are married. He doesn't want to hear any more, and bids her goodbye for now. As she leaves, Daisy comes to a full realization the beauty of her past experiences and the future ones to come ("On a Clear Day"—Streisand).

With John Richardson

In the Angel of Mercy orphanage

"Most moviegoers will probably regard *On a Clear Day You Can See Forever* as a personal triumph for Barbra Streisand. And with good reason. She is marvelous in it—deft with her lines as she switches effortlessly from a glamorous British beauty of the nineteenth century to a drab little New York college girl of today, equally authoritative in her movements and gestures to make both roles convincing and appealing, and in glorious voice. . . . For the first time on the screen, Streisand emerges as a person —and a very charming, attractive one—rather than as a star personality projecting a dazzling, but patently synthetic, tour-de-force."

ARTHUR KNIGHT,
Saturday Review

"*On a Clear Day You Can See Forever* . . . gives Miss Streisand a wonderful opportunity to wear all sorts of lavish costumes on all sorts of sumptuous sets and sing some tuneful ditties by Burton Lane and Alan Jay Lerner about flowers and ESP. . . . But there are times, alas, when she's not around, and that's when the movie around her falls right on its face. . . . I'd like to know whose suicidal idea it was to hire Yves Montand to play the romantic lead. Based on his past record in Hollywood movies, I'd say he has about as much drawing power as a dead walrus. . . . When he's not standing on top of the Pan Am Building, shot by helicopter with his arms outstretched, singing 'Bleest your hide, heer me cull, Must I fight City Hull, cum buck do mee' in his *boulevardier* style, he's announcing, 'Daisy, somewhere in yoo is zee keey to all zis!' It's all Miss Streisand can do to keep a straight face."

REX REED

"There is an odd magnetism to *On a Clear Day* that is hard to describe. In print, the plotline about the successive reincarnations of a Brooklyn 'little nobody' becomes pure soap opera. Praises of John De Cuir's lavish art direction and Vincente Minnelli's unobtrusive and old-fashioned (in the best sense of the word) direction do not fully capture the film's appeal. Barbra Streisand's lively performance and Yves Montand's warmly strong presence also do not account for the picture's success. In a very real way, this is a picture that has to be seen to be believed. . . ."

DEAC ROSSELL,
Boston After Dark

With Irene Handl

"Barbra Streisand is the queen of the movie musicals. Unfortunately, as evidenced by this film version of the Broadway show, her kingdom has been reduced to a duchy. Vincente Minnelli has mounted an old-fashioned production which begins promisingly enough with a magical blend of charm and whimsy but soon collapses under the weight of a creaky libretto and a cardboard leading man. Streisand, as Daisy Gamble, incessant smoker and minor-league soothsayer has polished her self-mocking style. She is undeniably beautiful and absolutely enchanting . . . her rendition of Alan Jay Lerner's bright and witty lyrics and Burton Lane's romantic music is pure and magnificent Streisand."

DONALD J. MAYERSON,
Cue

With Larry Blyden

"The high point of the film for me, and one of the most graceful Streisand moments ever put on film, is the royal dinner at which Minnelli's camera explores Miss Streisand in loving circling close-up while her voice is heard on the soundtrack singing 'Love With All the Trimmings.' . . . Nothing is allowed to get in the way of Miss Streisand, but Minnelli . . . has not been completely inhibited by her. He handles her gingerly (I have a feeling her comedy readings are all her own), but with an appreciation of her beauty and of the largely unrealized possibilities of her talent. Talent such as hers will not break when tested; it becomes enriched."

VINCENT CANBY
The New York Times

"Putting Miss Streisand in the dual role of Daisy Gamble/Melinda Tentrees was the movie's first, best and only inspiration. It's almost inspiration enough for awhile. She's alive and at home in any period, any accent the movie requires of her: the haughty, throaty refinement of an English lady, the Cockney chirpings of that lady's humble youth, the dejected plaints of a collegiate nicotine addict. She looks grand as Melinda, stroking her breast with a cool crystal goblet of white wine to arouse a man ogling her at dinner (the gambit would work equally well with red wine). She's a thoroughbred clotheshorse for Cecil Beaton's costumes. She flashes lightning-like between Melinda's airs and Daisy's earthiness, and when her Daisy admits to possession of various psychic powers—'I make flowers grow'—she does so ruefully, as if it were a curse and she were Mrs. Job."

Newsweek

"As an Englishwoman falling on her London derriere, Barbra is camp Joan Greenwood. As the clumsy American who washed her brain and can't do a thing with it, she is Jerry Lewis in drag. . . . Streisand ought to go back to playing Streisand. It is clear by now that she cannot be anyone else."

Time

"On a Clear Day You Can See Forever . . . is an absolute delight for Barbra Streisand fans, and a pleasure for even less passionate admirers of the lady, for here she has her major dramatic opportunity and makes the most of it. She is not only an extraordinarily gifted comedienne but a sensitive actress. . . . What a wallow for us Barbra buffs!"

JUDITH CRIST
New York

NOTES

Barbra's third film was a wonderful fantasy which many of her fans consider her finest effort.

The see-through outfit which Barbra wore to the 1969 Academy Awards was designed for this film, but was never used.

"So long, doctor—see ya later!"

A MAD MAGAZINE SATIRE

AS T. Byron Schmeer of Muncie, Indiana, once remarked to C. Fensterwick McCandless, of Hopatcong, New Jersey: "When you've seen one Barbra Streisand movie, you've seen them all!" With these immortal words ringing in our ears, we here at MAD now present, once and for all...

ARTIST: MORT DRUCKER

WRITER: FRANK JACOBS

ON A CLEA
GIRL SING

Hey, you kids! Bubby Strident is **singing** over the main title, and you're all **yelling** and **screaming** and **carrying on**!

Whatsa matter, Mister? Don't you ever sing along?!

I'v see thi pictu 31 tim

Class, I shall now demonstrate the **scientific value** of hypnosis by giving each of these subjects a **post-hypnotic suggestion** . . .

Mr. Jennings, when I clap my hands, you will awake, quack like a duck, jump like a frog, and eat like a horse . . .

Mr. Cooper, when I clap my hands you will awake, think you are an airplane, fly out the window of this 10-story building, bounce twice, and die . . .

Miss Vavoom, when I clap my hands, you will awake, go to my apartment, slip into something comfortable, and wait for me in a state of trembling ecstasy! Ah, **science!**

Ah, this student is in the **deepest** hypnotic trance I've ever seen! Who are you? And please don't sing me your answer—I want to **understand yo**

AY YOU CAN SEE A FUNNY "HELLO DOLLY" FOREVER

*Sung to the tune of "You Are Woman, I Am Man"

*Reprise—to the tune of "On A Clear Day You Can See Forever"

E OWL AND THE PUSSYCAT

Columbia Release of a Rastar Productions Picture
70). In Panavision and Eastmancolor. Rated R.

ST

ris	Barbra Streisand
x	George Segal
ney	Robert Klein
ss shop proprietor	Allen Garfield
mor	Roz Kelly
zinsky	Jacques Sandulescu
Weyderhaus	Jack Manning
. Weyderhaus	Grace Carney
s Weyderhaus	Barbara Anson
ater cashier	Kim Chan
tcheck man	Stan Gottlieb
man neighbor	Joe Madden
woman neighbor	Fay Sappington
ney's girl	Marilyn Briggs
n in bar	Dominic T. Barto
ng in car	Marshall Ward, Tom Atkins,
	Stan Bryant

EDITS

duced by	Ray Stark
ected by	Herbert Ross
eenplay by	Buck Henry
ed on the play	
he Owl and the Pussycat" by	Bill Manhoff
sented on the New York stage by	
	Philip Rose, Pat Fowler and
	Seven-Arts Productions.
otography by	Harry Stradling, A.S.C.
	Andrew Laszlo, A.S.C.
duction designer	John Robert Lloyd
directors	Robert Wightman,
	Philip Rosenberg
ted by	John F. Burnett
t production manager	Robert Greenhut
istant director	William C. Gerrity
decorator	Leif Pedersen
ipt supervisor	Marguerite James
duction assistant	Leo Garen
sic editor	William Saracino
nd	Arthur Piantadosi, Dennis Maitland
sic composed and arranged by	Richard Halligan
ics by	Blood, Sweat and Tears
formed by	Blood, Sweat and Tears
sign supervision by	Ken Adam
ke-up	Lee Harmon, Joe Cranzano
irstylist	Robert Grimaldi
rdrobe	Shirlee Strahm, George Newman
le design	Wayne Fitzgerald
stumes	Ann Roth
ting	Marion Dougherty
ervising film editor	Margaret Booth
ociate producer	George Justin

Doris is an actress and model who doesn't do much acting or modelling.

The ad campaign for The Owl and The Pussycat was one of the most amusing in movie history. Many variations on this theme were used. The ad above was used by newspapers which refused to run photographs of Doris's suggestive "modelling outfit" in its full detail.

In Doris' profession you have to know how to sell yourself.

Doris loses her job as a go-go dancer

With George Segal

SYNOPSIS

Felix Sherman (George Segal), a self-styled intellectual and would-be writer, informs his landlord about the late-night entertainment activities of one of his neighbors, Doris (Barbra Streisand). When Doris discovers who "squealed" and got her "thrown into the street," she cons her way into Felix's apartment and bombards him with vicious epithets, calling him a "pansy" and saying he is "jealous of what the big boys are doing." When he retorts that she is a whore, she insists that she "a model and an actress." Felix is convinced that she's crazy, but, desiring sleep, he agrees to let her spend the night in his apartment on the condition that she be long gone by morning.

Doris begins complaining, however, that she can't sleep without the TV on. Annoyed that Felix is ignoring her, she charges into his bedroom and discovers him undressed. His outraged modesty at this so amuses her th she has an uncontrollable fit of hiccups. She tells Felix th the only way she can get rid of them is for him to frighten her. After several unsuccessful attempts at this l Felix, she goes to the kitchen for a drink. In the meantim Felix puts on a Halloween skeleton costume, and he frightens her so much that the noise she makes gets them both thrown out of the building.

They take refuge in the apartment of one of Felix's co-workers (Robert Klein). Doris continues to demand TV set and Felix, desperate for sleep, puts a show on for her from behind a fish tank. This only serves to make Doris anxious to hear one of his stories. He finally agrees to read her one, but his overblown imagery infuriates he and she tells him she hates his writing. They begin anoth verbal battle, which drives Felix's friend to leave his own apartment for someplace quieter.

Alone now in the apartment, Doris attempts to sed Felix and, after several rebuffs, she succeeds. Their love-making is a comedy of errors, with Doris calling the sho and Felix telling her to let him do things his way. After-ward, Doris is finally able to sleep. The next morning, Felix asks Doris about her previous sexual partners, and she is incensed. Still another shouting match ensues, after which she storms out of the apartment, blasting his writ-ing again. As she leaves, Felix calls her a "streetwalker."

The next few days provide time for Doris and Felix to think about each other. Felix takes the opportunity to see one of Doris's films, an epic entitled Cycle Sluts. Before long, they're re-united, and Felix tries to explain himself to Doris. She, to please him, has bought a the-saurus, with which she hopes to "assimilate five new wor a day." Felix takes her to the apartment of his fiancée's parents, which is empty. They are taking a bath togethe when Felix's future in-laws, the Weyderhauses (Jack Manning and Grace Carney), enter. The situation is further complicated when Doris recognizes Mr. Wey-derhaus as one of her regular customers. After fleeing th house, Doris and Felix have their most brutal argument. After attempting to humiliate Doris, Felix throws away typewriter and admits that he is really Fred Sherman, a bookstore clerk. Doris tells him that she was "formerly hooker," and they walk off together, honest with each other and themselves for the first time.

With George Segal

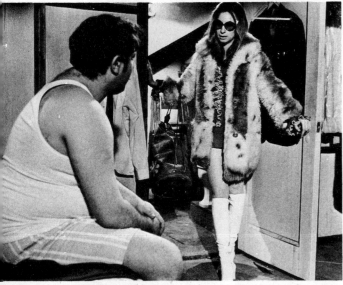

George Segal, as Felix, attends one of Doris's epics.

REVIEWS

"With *The Owl and the Pussycat*, we can resume th
inspection and the enjoyment of the real Barbra Streisand
In a sense we haven't seen her since she was Miss Marmel
stein in *I Can Get It For You Wholesale*. In *Funny Gir*
both on stage and in the movie, she was partly herself, bu
partly overwhelmed by a waxen vehicle that only she, th
first of the red hot daughters, could have melted throug
and in *Hello, Dolly!* and *On a Clear Day You Can S*
Forever, she was forced to manipulate her personality an
talent like some inspired Silly Putty in order to outfac
the elephantine exigencies of those big deals.

"But now all the circus junk and the mastodon dro
pings have been cleared away and we have Streisand plai
There she comes, right where she belongs, in a real Ne
York street, ducking through the sleazy rain in a fake-f
minicoat, white boots scrambling, tote bag swinging, cus
ing out a departing bus in her interborough voice an
with a shrug and a chomp on her Juicy Fruit, floppi
into a passing car. That's the way girls used to come in
our movies, and our fantasies, and it's about time
remembered that Streisand is the latest of our girls—o
Normands, Lombards, Harlows, Blondells, Monroes."

JACK KROL
Newswe

George Segal

193

With George Segal

"In any compilation of the modern world's ten most
rewarding stunts, the casting of Barbra Streisand in a
light comedy, especially one as flimsily fabricated as
Owl and the Pussycat, must rank close to Charles A.
Cohen's 1920 attempt to ride over Niagara Falls in a
barrel, which turned out to be fatal.

"Miss Streisand survives . . . but largely on goodwill,
because, even though she never sings, it's possible to
remember what happens when she does: through the force
of mysterious, implacable talent, she goes a long way
toward making one agree that she is—as she proclaimed in
Funny Girl, with an immense desire to please—the greatest star. Without a song, she simply isn't. There is still that
immense desire to please, but it now seems rooted in bellig-
erency, rather than vulnerability. As Doris Waverly/
Wadsworth/Wellington (née Wilgus), a very improbable New York hooker with a heart of gold, Miss Streisand,
a straight comedienne, lacks one essential feature—
namely a heart. The performance, which may owe a lot to
the manner in which it was written (by Buck Henry) and
directed (by Herbert Ross), is mostly cold and edgy and
aggressive and loud. There are odd, but only occasional
moments—when she suddenly smiles a genuine smile, or
when she is listening to someone other than herself (for a
change)—that recall, if distantly, the real, feeling, thinking
performer whose soul is in her music."

VINCENT CANBY,
The New York Times

"In her first non-singing role, Miss Streisand emerges
on her own, demonstrating the variety and depth of the
dramatic talents that were indicated but unexploited in her
musical roles. She has all the brass of a street urchin, the
toughness of the survivor and the tawdriness of the tramp
in the exterior Doris . . . but it is the interior Doris, with
the sharp mind and the tender heart, that makes her characterization valid, that justifies the loud mouth and bra-
zen behavior. In her performance, Miss Streisand is as
chameleonic as her face and she provides a variety of tem-
perament and countenance that makes her role a delight
that last even for non-Barbra addicts."

JUDITH CRIST,
New York

"Segal gives a fine, subtle, comic performance in a
film that is anything but subtle, and opposite an all-stops-
out display of fireworks by La Streisand. She doesn't sing,
but she does every other bit of shtick and business that
writer Buck Henry and director Herbert Ross could cram
into one film. She is alternately crude, witty, bawdy and
hilarious, and so is the film."

GAIL ROCK,
Women's Wear Daily

". . . It's surprising, at least to me, that it is still possible to resurrect the moldy delusion of the whore with a
golden heart, build a comedy around it and get away with
it. The reason it all works is simply Barbra Streisand, who
. . . is terrifically funny in *The Owl and the Pussycat*,
which for her is a triumph of talent over material. Her
familiar mannerisms, her timing, her apparent sense of
what's funny and what's not set her apart and make her
possibly the most effective comedienne working in films.
Hers is not a subtle drawing room attack, but then *The
Owl and the Pussycat* is hardly Noël Coward."

JOE ROSEN,
New York Morning Telegraph

"*The Owl and The Pussycat* is a cheering, satisfying
romantic comedy . . . the material is far from first rate, but
it's functional. Like some of the thin and totally concocted
screwball comedies of the thirties, it draws its life from
the performers. Streisand, self-conscious and self-mocking,
combative but wistful, is an intuitive actress who needs
someone to play against . . . she and Segal have the temperamental affinity to make a romantic comedy take off.
Their rapport has a beautiful, worked-out professionalism.
Were Hepburn and Tracy this good together, even at
their best, as in *Pat and Mike*? Maybe, but they weren't
better."

PAULINE KAEL,
The New Yorker

NOTE

Barbra's favorite cameraman, Harry Stradling, died
during the filming of this movie.

*Doris and Felix enjoy a bath in the home of his
fiancee until she and her parents interrupt (with
Barbara Anson, Jack Manning and Grace Carney)*

a screwball comedy. ★ Remember Them?

Barbra Streisand ★ Ryan O'Neal
"What's Up Doc?"
A Peter Bogdanovich Production

BARBRA STREISAND · RYAN O'NEAL in "WHAT'S UP, DOC?" A Peter Bogdanovich Production · Co-Starring KENNETH MARS
AUSTIN PENDLETON · SORRELL BOOKE · MICHAEL MURPHY · And Introducing MADELINE KAHN · Screenplay by
Buck Henry and David Newman & Robert Benton · Story by Peter Bogdanovich · Directed and Produced by Peter Bogdanovich
TECHNICOLOR® From Warner Bros., A Warner Communications Company [G] ALL AGES ADMITTED General Audiences

WHAT'S UP, DOC?

A Warner Brothers Release of a Saticoy Picture
(1972). In Technicolor. Rated G.

CAST

Judy Maxwell	Barbra Streisand
Howard Bannister	Ryan O'Neal
Hugh Simon	Kenneth Mars
Frederick Larrabee	Austin Pendleton
Harry	Sorrell Booke
Fritz	Stefan Gierasch
Mrs. Van Hoskins	Mabel Albertson
Mr. Smith	Michael Murphy
Bailiff	Graham Jarvis
Eunice Burns	Madeline Kahn
The Judge	Liam Dunn
Mr. Jones	Phil Roth
Mr. Kaltenborn	John Hillerman
Rudy, the headwaiter	George Morfogen
Prof. Hosquith	Randy Quaid
Arresting officer	M. Emmett Walsh
Banquet receptionist	Eleanor Zee
Delivery boy	Kevin O'Neal

CREDITS

Produced and directed by	Peter Bogdanovich
Screenplay by	
	Buck Henry, David Newman and Robert Ben
Photography by	Laszlo Kovacs
Production designer	Polly Platt
Art director	Herman A. Blumenthal
Edited by	Verna Fields
Sound by	Les Fresholtz
Script supervisor	Hazel Hall
Set decorator	John Austin
Special effects	Robert MacDonald
Titles	The Gold West, Inc.
Associate producer	Paul Lewis
Music arranged and conducted by	Artie Butler
Unit production manager	Fred Ahern
Assistant to producer	Frank Marshall
Makeup supervisor	Don Cash
Hairstylist	Lynda Gurasich
Men's costume supervision	Nancy McArdle
Assistant film editor	William Neel
Assistant director	Ray Gosnell
Publicist	Carl Combs

With Ryan O'Neal

SYNOPSIS

Judy Maxwell (Barbra Streisand), an eccentric near-genius who has been thrown out of every university she ever attended (she can't recall the number), meets Howard Bannister (Ryan O'Neal), a stuffy young musicologist, in San Francisco. Howard has come to that city to attend a convention at which he hopes to win a $20,000 prize for a strange primitive music theory he has formulated. Attracted to Howard, Judy thrusts herself upon him with single-minded zeal, despite the disconcerting presence of Howard's fiancée, Eunice Burns (Madeline Kahn), who is probably the world's biggest drag. Judy and Howard become involved in several irrational mix-ups, one involving four identical plaid overnight cases. In hers, Judy carries her clothes and an encyclopedia. Howard's contains rare igneous rocks essential to proving his theory. The other two cases belong to Mrs. Van Hoskins (Mabel Albertson) and Mr. Smith (Michael Murphy). Mrs. Van Hoskins' case contains a fortune in jewels. Mr. Smith's contains secret government papers, and he is being followed by Mr. Jones (Phil Roth), who wants them.

All of these individuals are staying at the San Francisco Hilton, on the seventeenth floor. The crooked hotel detective Harry (Sorrell Booke) and Fritz, the desk clerk (Stefan Gierasch), are trying to steal Mrs. Van Hoskins' jewels. At the same time, Mr. Jones is trying to get Mr. Smith's secret papers. No one particularly wants Judy's clothes or Howard's rocks, but confusion reigns as cases are stolen, hidden and lost by all involved.

At the convention, Judy poses as Howard's fiancée. The head of the foundation which is offering the $20,000 prize, Mr. Larrabee (Austin Pendleton), finds Judy (whom he thinks is Eunice) charming, and Howard finally gives up trying to explain that she isn't really his fiancée. Meanwhile, the real Eunice is trying to enter the ballroom, but since Judy had picked up her identification badge, she is not allowed in. She finally storms into the banquet and demands that Howard tell who she is. He, in something of a daze by now, denies ever seeing her before. She is dragged out, screaming.

Also present at the convention is a nasty fellow named Simon (Kenneth Mars), who is competing with Howard for the award. Later, Simon discovers that Judy is not Howard's fiancée, and he sees his chance to discredit

Howard and assure himself the award. Meanwhile, Judy has gotten into Howard's room and is taking a bubble bath when he discovers her. When he tries to hide her so that Eunice, with whom he is attempting to make up, will not realize she is there, pandemonium breaks out. A fire results in Howard's room, and he is asked to leave the hotel.

On the set.

A party is scheduled at which Mr. Larrabee is to announce the winner of the prize. Judy overhears Harry giving an address to someone, and, posing on the phone as Mr. Larrabee's secretary, uses it to steer Eunice to the wrong place. She then attends the party, again posing as Howard's fiancée. Simon attempts to inform Larrabee of Judy's true identity, but is continually thwarted. When Eunice arrives at the address Judy gave her, she finds it, to say the least, run-down. She discovers several hoodlums who are unhappy that they didn't get the case with the jewels. "What are you doing with Howard Bannister's rocks?" asks Eunice, and the hoodlums take her by force to Larrabee's.

Finally, everyone converges on the party and, in the confusion, Judy and Howard escape with the four cases, just to make sure one of them contains Howard's rocks. A wild chase begins, with the pair on a grocer's cart, and the rest in hot pursuit in a taxi and a convertible. The chase involves them with ladders, a huge pane of glass, a Chinese dragon, a cement layer and a plunge into San Francisco Bay.

They all wind up in front of the world's most harried judge (Liam Dunn), who looks at the assembled mass of humanity and says, "Let's get this horror show on the road." The judge just happens to be Judy's father. Finally, Howard, who has been left by Eunice in favor of Mr. Larrabee, begins to head back to Ames, Iowa. He learns that Simon has won the award by default, since Howard is considered by the foundation to be an unstable personality. But Judy distantly recalls the details of Simon's theory, and Larrabee realizes that Simon is a plagiarist. Howard is given the prize money, but after paying his share of the extensive damages the group wrought on San Francisco, he is left with very little except Judy, who follows him onto the plane and convinces him that they belong together.

REVIEWS

"Not the least of Bogdanovich's success in scaling down Miss Streisand's superstar personality to fit the dimensions of farce. Although she never lets forget the power that always seems to be held in uncertain check, she is surprisingly appealing, more truly comic than she's ever before been on film. Bogdanovich has also had the good sense to allow her to sing at least twice, once under the titles (a smashing arrangement of Porter's 'You're the Top') and once in the film itself ('As Time Goes By')."

VINCENT CANBY
The New York Times

"Streisand sings a sizzling version of 'You're the Top' behind the titles, and there's a moment in the movie when the audience cheers as she starts to sing 'As Time Goes By,' but it's just a teaser, and it has to last for the whole movie. Why? Nothing that happens in the movie—none of the chases or comic confusions—has the excitement of her singing. When a tiger pretends to be a pussycat, that's practically a form of Uncle Tomism. Yes, she's more easily acceptable in *What's Up, Doc?* than in her bigger roles, because she doesn't tap her full talent and there is an element of possible unpleasantness, of threat, in that real hot talent—as there is in Liza Minnelli at full star strength—which produces unresolved feelings in us. It's easy to see that those people who haven't liked Streisand before could like her this time, because here her charm has no drive. . . ."

PAULINE KAEL
The New Yorker

Ryan O'Neal, Austin Pendleton and Kenneth Mars

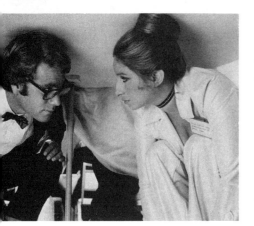

With Ryan O'Neal

Madeline Kahn, Austin Pendleton, Ryan O'Neal and Phil Roth in court.

The chase sequence (with Ryan O'Neal)

"About the stars: Ryan O'Neal comes off like Cary Grant's stand-in—no more, no less. Streisand remains an original with the canny of a kid from Brooklyn on the make; she's one of the biggest talents to hit the screen, and if this film doesn't do much to enlarge her reputation, at least it doesn't damage it. I found it her least effective film to date."

LARRY COHEN,
Show

"When *What's Up, Doc?* is good, it is very fine indeed. Streisand is a nimble comedienne who is especially winning when she lounges atop a piano mimicking Humphrey Bogart and singing 'As Time Goes By' from *Casablanca*. Ryan O'Neal is no Cary Grant, but for someone basically miscast in the role of the bumblesome, studious chap who has a great deal of trouble with doorknobs and bow ties, he displays an engagingly light touch and is enormously appealing. The supporting cast is like a perfectly matched set of colored croquet balls bouncing off the stars in brilliantly diagrammed cameos. . . ."

REX REED

"Miss Streisand knows no subtleties in her comedy craft. She is an outrageous mugger. Nothing is done in low key. The opening scene in which she pursues O'Neal in a hotel drug store is painfully bad. Sometimes she attempts softness in her love scenes but the brassiness of the preceding moment drowns it out. Miss Streisand's competition in the comedienne field are Lucille Ball and Carol Burnett. She could learn a great deal from them. In *Doc*, her competition is Madeline Kahn, who plays O'Neal's fiancée. She is extremely funny by being exaggerated without losing the shape of a real character. This is what Miss Streisand can't do because she is basically a variety performer, not a movie star. The qualities that make a Marilyn Monroe a Movie Star, from looks to timing, are not evident in Miss Streisand's film roles."

BRUCE BAHRENBURG,
Newark Evening News

"Despite all the publicity about the off-camera frissons between the stars, Ryan and Barbra are surprisingly flat in their scenes together. O'Neal seems to be reading his lines off cue cards, and they're not very funny lines in the first place. Writers Buck Henry, David Newman and Robert Benton have given all the truly funny dialogue to the supporting players."

GAIL ROCK,
Women's Wear Daily

"Comedy, more than other genres, depends on the performances of the actors; and this film is blessed with an abundance of gems. Streisand, minus her Flatbush twang, is wacky, campy, and endearing—her best performance to date."

JOHN BROECK,
The Villager

UP THE SANDBOX

A First Artists Presentation of a Barwood Film.
A National General Release (1972). In
Technicolor. Rated R.

CAST

Margaret	Barbra Streisand
Paul	David Selby
Elizabeth	Ariane Heller
Peter	Terry/Garry Smith
Mrs. Yussim	Jane Hoffman
Mr. Yussim	John C. Becher
Fidel Castro	Jacobo Morales
Dr. Beineke	Paul Benedict
Dr. Keglin	George Irving
Mrs. Keglin	Jane House
Uncle Dave	Pitt Herbert
Aunt Ida	Janet Brandt
Aunt Till	Pearl Shear
Vinnie	Carl Gottlieb
John	Joseph Bova
Betty	Mary Louise Wilson
Judy	Marilyn Curtis
Vicki	Iris Brooks
Bibs	Tammy Lee
Becky	Randy Ginns
Tommy	Stanley Appleman
Billy	Moosie Drier
Nanny	Jessamine Milner
Stella	Cynthia Harris
David	Mark Vahanian
Jack Lawford	Vassili Lambrinos
Dr. Lopez	Marina Durrell
Dr. Boden	Barbara Rhodes
Maria	Isabel Sanford
Miss Spittlemeister	Carol White
Leon	Danny Black
John (Black Militant)	David Downing
Black captain	Ji-Tu Cumbuka
Black man	Juan DeCarlos
Statue of Liberty guard	Paul Dooley
Dr. Gordon	Conrad Bain
Woman doctor	Jane Betts
Battleaxe	Anne Ramsey
Hospital clerk	Margo Winkler
Woman patient	Cryn Matchinga
Officer	John Dennis
Reporter	Norman Field
Castro's aide	Efrain Lopez Neris
Elinore	Lois Smith
Elinor's boy	Steven Britt
Connie	Renee Lippin
Cathie	Terry O'Mara
Joanne	Jennifer Darling
Judy Stanley	Stockard Channing
Mrs. Grossbard	Rita Karin
Rose White	Marilyn Coleman
Black girl	Dee Timberlake
Pro-Cuban	Alicia Castroleal
Anti-Cuban	Juan Canos
Clay	Conrad Roberts
Boy on bike	Kevin Bersell
Fat man	Sully Boyer
Jan	Lee Chamberlain
African chieftess	Miriam W'Abdullah
Gupa	Beth Luzuka
Dancers	National Senegalese Dance Company
Tribal population	Somburu Tribe of Kenya

CREDITS

Producers	Irwin Winkler and Robert Chartoff
Associate producer	Marty Erlichman
Director	Irvin Kershner
Writer	Paul Zindel
Executive in charge of production	Hal Polaire
Production manager (New York)	Jerry Shapiro
Production coordinator (Kenya)	Eva Monley
Production assistant	Jeff Benjamin
Production coordinator (New York)	Ralph Singleton
First assistant director	Howard W. Koch, Jr.
Director of photography	Gordon Willis
Photographic consultant	Bernard Abramson
Camera operator	Jack Whitman
Sound mixer	Lawrence O. Jost
Script supervisor	Betty Crosby
Production designer	Harry Horner
Set decorator	Robert De Vestel
Set designer	David M. Haber
Special effects	Richard F. Albain
Publicist	Harry Mines
Wardrobe designer	Albert Wolsky
Costume supervisor	Lambert Marks
Hairstylist	Kaye Pownell
Make-up man	Lee C. Harman
Casting	Cis Corman
Film editor	Robert Lawrence
Assistant editor	Norman Suffern

SYNOPSIS

Margaret Reynolds (Barbra Streisand) is a Manhattan housewife with two children and a brilliant professor husband, Paul (David Selby). She also has a domineering mother (Jane Hoffman) who insists that Margaret leave the "slum" she's living in and move near her family in New Jersey.

Margaret loves her husband and children, but she's discontented. She needs more than being a housewife, mother, maid, nurse, baby-sitter and laundrywoman. To make matters worse, she's just learned she's pregnant again. Unable to escape her mundane existence, Margaret fantasizes herself in various strange and wonderful situations.

Her first fantasy involves one of her husband's attractive young female colleagues, Dr. Boden (Barbara Rhodes). Margaret asks her if she is having an affair with Paul, and she answers, "Why yes, of course." The scene ends in a happy embrace as Dr. Boden tells Margaret that Paul has often professed his love for his wife.

After meeting an old college professor of hers in Latin American Studies, Margaret imagines herself riling Fidel Castro (Jacobo Morales) at a press conference. Castro then has her brought to his hotel suite, where he reveals to her his amazing secret: he is actually a woman.

After awakening from this dream, Margaret is visited by her mother, whom she briefly imagines breaking into her apartment against her protests. As Mrs. Yussim nags her once again to buy a house in New Jersey, Margaret leaves the apartment with her children and heads for the park. There, her imagination takes her on a desperate mission with Black revolutionaries to blow up the Statue of Liberty. After lighting fuses of dynamite sticks, Margaret sees Paul running to the top to commit suicide. She attempts to save him, and both perish as the Statue crashes into New York Harbor.

Several days later, at an anniversary party for her parents, Margaret is annoyed as her mother tries to convince Paul that moving to New Jersey is what his wife

With Jacobo Morales

204

y wants. Margaret envisions herself finally standing up
er mother, telling her exactly what she thinks of her
dling, pushing her face into the anniversary cake and
y battling her to the finish on the floor as the
e-movie cameras roll.

Frustrations and self-doubts continue to pile up for
garet at home. During a party, she is upset by Paul's
tion to a full-bosomed young blonde. She soon sees
elf as hugely pregnant and, retiring to a bedroom,
es her stomach in until she suddenly develops
ptuous breasts. Letting her hair down, she returns to
arty to wow her husband. When he doesn't notice
new figure, her ego and bosom are both equally
ated.

Paul's attention to the blonde causes a huge fight,
wing which Margaret imagines herself on a trip to the
besi River in Africa, to discover the Somburu tribe's
od of painless childbirth. There she and her guide,
Beineke (Paul Benedict) are killed for attempting to
ver this sacred secret.

Back in the laundryroom where this fantasy began,
garet collapses. Being cared for later by Paul and her
her, she imagines telling Paul she wants more children
a house full of noise and happiness. Paul's response is a
ent rejection of the whole idea, and he screams at her
l she is forced to jump out of the window.

After asking Paul for "the day off," Margaret's final
asy takes place. She visualizes herself in an abortion
c, with Paul frantically trying to stop her. After
ing out of this dream, Margaret joins her husband and
dren at an amusement park. Between spins of a
usel, she tells Paul that she's pregnant, and they
de it really is a blessed event. The story ends with
garet riding off in a taxi to enjoy her day away from
responsibilities.

Margaret argues with Fidel Castro

With David Selby

Filming the Statue of Liberty sequence.

One of Margaret's fantasies (with Jane Hoffman)

"Barbra Streisand adds another accomplishment to [ ] many with a superb display of acting. In this touchi[ ] funny, exhilarating and mature movie set in New Yo[ ] Miss Streisand creates a remarkable portrait of a wife a[ ] mother of two, who discovers she is pregnant at a ti[ ] when she is concerned with the value of women—to m[ ] and to themselves.

"Streisand's Walter Mitty vignettes—working w[ ] Black revolutionaries to blow up the Statue of Liberty, [ ] rebelling against an officious mother—are gems of hum[ ] and insight. This is a fine film and an important one in [ ] treatment of female versus femininity."

DONALD J. MAYERSO[ ]
C[ ]

"Even with a few arid patches and fantasies t[ ] unwind a bit methodically at times, Barbra Streisan[ ] sixth film is her sixth hit. Yes, think of it. An hour af[ ] seeing this new one, which is ripe, yeasty fun, it's hard n[ ] to think of this extraordinary woman, perfectly wedded [ ] the camera with her instant Modigliani face and timi[ ] She's the picture, true, but the teamwork is admirab[ ] Nearly everything works and meshes . . . even wh[ ] they're way out, the vignette musings generally m[ ] blandness and strain because our heroine is a bright, lika[ ] girl, not a pinhead."

HOWARD THOMPSO[ ]
The New York Tim[ ]

"*Up the Sandbox* . . . unfortunately is a confusi[ ] comedy. The screen adaptation of Paul Zindel, who wro[ ] *The Effect of Gamma Rays on Man-in-the-Moon Ma[ ] golds*, jumps from reality to fantasy in the same uncle[ ] fashion as Ann Richardson Roiphe's book upon which t[ ] film is based. The result is a jumbled story line."

ANN GUARIN[ ]
New York Daily Ne[ ]

On location in Africa

"The only force that holds *Up the Sandbox* together
 arbra's magnetism, although the Star does not tran-
 d the movie as say, Bette Davis did in *Beyond the
 st*, where despite the studio quarrels, miscasting, and
 writing, Bette managed to show herself off to best
 t is bitchiest) advantage. Now, there's no question
 Barbra could, if she wanted to, transport the whole
 duction over the Hollywood rainbow. After all, isn't
 ra the original kid from Flatbush who could wiseguy
 body into buying the Brooklyn Bridge? It's just that in
 the Sandbox, the superstar chose to stroll her role,
 ng a very soft sell. (Come on, Babs, you could maybe
 e sung a title song or something!) But why pick?
 isand is Streisand and, like Dietrich or Garbo, can
 er really fail on screen even if she is cast in a hundred
 -crap quickies like *Up the Sandbox*. For Barbra cultists
 ."

JOHN CALENDO,
Inter/View

"Barbra Streisand lovable? Surprisingly, yes, and after
 the Sandbox it might be difficult to think otherwise.
 s refreshing, imaginative and tenderly moving comedy
 vides her with her finest role to date and she rises to the
 llenge cunningly. To call her performance as a Man-
 an housewife . . . a total departure is not entirely true.
 bra has always fused in her work opposing elements of
 w-biz razzmatazz and recognizable femininity . . . but
 re is new vulnerability in her work here, a touching
 etness that makes you want to know the character
 ead of the actress. The maturity, the depth and the
 on she has achieved as a woman and an actress are
 ly joyous to observe."

REX REED

"As Streisand's pictures multiply, it becomes apparent
 t she is not about to master an actress's craft but,
 her, is discovering a craft of her own, out of the timing
 emotionality that make her a phenomenon as a singer.
 admire her not for her acting—or singing—but for
 self, which is what you feel she gives you in both. She
 the class to be herself, and the impudent music of her
 aking voice is proof that she knows it. The audacity of
 self-creation is something we've had time to adjust to;
 already know her mettle, and the dramatic urgency she
 bring to roles. In *Up the Sandbox*, she shows a much
 per and warmer presence and a fully yielding qual-
 . . ."

JUDITH CRIST,
New York

With David Selby and her film children

THE WAY WE WERE

A Columbia Pictures and Rastar Productions
Presentation (1973). In Panavision. Rated PG.

CAST

Katie	Barbra Streisand
Hubbell	Robert Redford
J.J.	Bradford Dillman
Carol Ann	Lois Chiles
George Bissinger	Patrick O'Neal
Paula Reisner	Viveca Lindfors
Rhea Edwards	Allyn Ann McLerie
Brooks Carpenter	Murray Hamilton
Bill Verso	Herb Edelman
Vicki Bissinger	Diana Ewing
Pony Dunbar	Sally Kirkland
Peggy Vanderbilt	Marcia Mae Jones
Actor	Don Keefer
El Morocco captain	George Gaynes
Army corporal	Eric Boles
Ash blonde	Barbara Peterson
Army captain	Roy Jensen
Rally speaker	Brendan Kelly
Frankie McVeigh	James Woods
Jenny	Connie Forslund
Dr. Short	Robert Gerringer
Judianne	Susie Blakely
Airforce	Ed Power
Dumb blonde	Suzanne Zenor
Guest	Dan Seymour

CREDITS

Produced by	Ray Stark
Directed by	Sydney Pollack
Written by	Arthur Laurents
Director of photography	Harry Stradling, Jr., A.S.C.
Production designer	Stephen Grimes
Supervising film editor	Margaret Booth
Associate producer	Richard Roth
Music by	Marvin Hamlisch
Song "The Way We Were"	composed by Marvin Hamlisch
	Lyrics by Marilyn and Alan Bergman
	Sung by Barbra Streisand
Unit production manager	Russ Saunders
Costume designers	Dorothy Jeakins, Moss Mabry
Script supervisor	Betty Crosby
Titles	Phill Norman
Set decorator	William Kiernan
Properties	Richard M. Rubin
Music editor	Ken Runyan
Assistant director	Howard Koch, Jr.
Second assistant director	Jerry Ziesmer
Make-up	Donald Cash, Jr. Gary Liddiard
Hairstyles	Kaye Pownell
Sound	Jack Solomon
Sound effects	Kay Rose
Re-recording	Richard Portman
Unit publicist	Carol Shapiro

Katie the activist rushes to class

With James Woods

At the prom (with Robert Redford and James Woods)

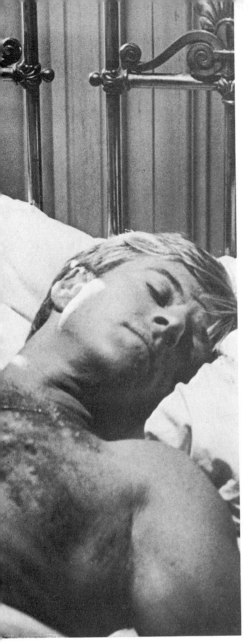

With Robert Redford

SYNOPSIS

In the late 1930s, Katie Morosky (Barbra Streisand) and Hubbell Gardiner (Robert Redford) are college classmates. Jewish Katie is a radical activist, a member of the Young Communist League, and totally devoid of humor when it comes to politics. Hubbell is a WASP, active in college sports and social life, unconcerned with political issues. His one ambition is to be a writer.

Working as a waitress near campus, Katie is the butt of jokes from Hubbell's friends. He, however, is kinder and later talks to her about the sale of his first short story. During a college formal, he dances briefly with her, and it is clear that he finds her interesting, and she finds him fascinating.

Several years later, Katie is broadcasting radical pronouncements, and Hubbell is in the service. At New York's El Morocco nightclub, they meet again. He is dead drunk, and Katie takes him to her apartment. After he undresses and gets into bed, she expectantly does the same. He makes a few encouraging overtures, but soon falls sound asleep.

The next morning, Katie prepares an elaborate breakfast, but Hubbell is too hung-over to even attempt to eat it. As he prepares to leave, she quickly gives him several phone numbers where she can be reached, and invites him to return whenever he is in town and needs a place to stay.

He eventually does call, and they spend an evening together at Katie's. She surprises him with a copy of a book he had had published several years earlier, and he is flattered. They discuss his writing and he becomes aware of Katie's sincere interest in his work. They begin dating frequently. But Hubbell's friends soon create problems. They continue to make jokes about the political issues Katie feels strongly about, and she considers them a group of asses. She continually creates scenes at parties by telling them off. Finally Hubbell decides to break off the romance. Katie wins him back by tearfully explaining that she only wants the best for him. They marry and move to California, where Hubbell is to turn his novel into a screenplay. Katie protests that he is too good a writer for Hollywood, and should continue writing his new novel. But he insists, and she gives in.

In Hollywood, things go well until the Red Scare of the post-War years threatens to destroy the film writers' community. Katie insists on going to Washington to protest the Un-American Activities Committee's hearings, despite Hubbell's protests and her pregnancy. Upon her return, an ugly scene is created at the train station by a mob screaming epithets at all those who defend the "Commies."

This problem, and Katie's attempts to fight it, put a terrible strain on the marriage. Things go badly for Hubbell at work, as well. The film's producers make major changes in Hubbell's script, and he feels himself losing control of his work. He begins to feel that he is committing the sell-out Katie had warned him against. Confused and depressed, Hubbell spends a night with his ex-girlfriend, whom Katie contemptuously describes as "Beekman Place." She discovers his infidelity, and is heartbroken that he should seek solace from someone she considers so shallow. They have a confrontation and sadly realize that their marriage is irreparable. They agree to part after the birth of their baby.

Years later, in New York City, Katie and Hubbell accidentally meet on the street. He has become a TV writer, and she has remarried. They painfully exchange the latest facts. Still very much in love, they have no delusions that they can ever be happy together. Hubbell tells her, "You'll never change" as Katie leaves him and begins passing out "Ban the Bomb" literature.

211

"*The Way We Were* . . . is everything a movie ould be: a love story that is a mirror of the hearts of any, a comedy that teeters on the edge of tragedy, a agedy that teeters on the edge of comedy. Due to the sting, which is nothing short of masterful, the film is stly superior to the Arthur Laurents novel on which it is sed. Barbra Streisand, as Katie, the ugly duckling college udent who majors in leftist causes and later, as the same atie, now an attractive young matron who tries vainly to nange her basic nature to please the college sweetheart e has married, gives the kind of dramatic performance f which Academy Award nominations are made . . . The easure of the success of this brilliant motion picture is at it draws the viewer so deeply into its web of charac- r and plot that one is so involved in the dreams and dis- pointments of its principals that one leaves the theatre eling as one often does when close to a couple who sorts to divorce—wondering 'Which one was right? Vhich one should I see in the future?' See both Katie and ubbell again. In *The Way We Were*. It's worth it."

NORMA McLAIN STOOP,
After Dark

Katie and Hubbell in Hollywood (with Robert Redford)

"The only thing that limits Barbra Streisand as a novie superstar is that she's not really an actress, not even nuch of a comedienne. She's an impersonator. When the npersonation fits the contours of the public personality —tough, driving, ambitious, shrewd, self-mocking—the erformance can be effective as it was in *Funny Girl*, and s it is for a short space of time in her new film . . . *The Vay We Were* looks like a 747 built around an elephant. t seems to have been constructed of prefabricated parts hat were then bolted together as best they could, consid- ring the nature of the cargo. . . . The Streisand talent is uge, eccentric and intractable. When she goes one way nd the movie goes another, it's no contest. The movie is urned into junk.

"The early sequences of the movie are not at all bad. The period detail, though heavily laid on, is funny and vocative. More importantly, it is easy to understand why hese two mismatched people could be so drawn to each other. Miss Streisand's furious determination is never very ppealing but it is comprehensible, as is Redford's essential veakness. . . . The love affair, the movie and Miss Streis- nd's performance all go wrong when the story follows he now-married couple to post-war Hollywood. . . . By ome peculiar alchemy, *The Way We Were* turns into he kind of compromised claptrap that Hubbell is sup- osed to be making within the film and that we're meant o think is a sellout. It is."

VINCENT CANBY,
The New York Times

With Robert Redford

With Robert Redford, Bradford Dillman, Patrick O'Neal and Viveca Lindfors at Marx Brothers costume party.

With Lois Chiles, Bradford Dillman, Robert Redford and Allyn Ann McLerie

On location in New York

"Pollack and Laurents are so busy working on the dubious proposition that politics can kill a good marriage that they barely have time to establish the political atmosphere that is meant as a catalyst to the connubial collapse, sketching it in hurriedly in bits of cocktail gossip and snippets of radio reports and newspaper headlines. Meanwhile, we watch this luxurious vehicle flounder and finally crack apart. Superb performances by Redford and Streisand are not enough to sustain our hopes for the kind of glamorous, big-star romance that Hollywood rarely attempts any more."

PAUL D. ZIMMERMAN,
Newsweek

"*The Way We Were* is almost a milestone because it's a thoughtful, believable love story for adults. For once, the characters are sharply defined, and their relationship develops and deepens persuasively . . . The differences that attract them will ultimately separate them; but there is real electricity between them . . . Some of the electrictiy comes from the two stars; their chemistry keeps the movie engaging. Streisand is still too shrill at moments; but this is the most forceful, controlled acting she's ever done. Redford is superb. . . ."

STEPHEN FARBER,
The New York Times (Sunday)

"Nobody could actually have been these glossy, unreal Hollywoodized characters. . . . Barbra Streisand and Robert Redford do have charisma and they can carry any film a long way, even this one, where they are smothered in clichés and banalities, from character conception to dialogue. . . . Dealing with the blacklisting is long overdue in films, but the mawkish unconvincing dabbling in persecution and protest as a background for this dumb tear-jerking love affair is shallow shadow-boxing."

WILLIAM WOLF,
Cue

"You have to say that the picture walks routinely down the dead center of the remembered path, with good and standard performances, and dialogues that are a veritable least common denominator of what was being said in all those days. In fact, the picture is so carefully put together as research that it lacks some of the accident and spontaneity of real life. . . . Redford and Streisand play their native types with accustomed mastery. You can choose either or both according to your taste. Streisand-haters will be relieved to know that on this occasion she does not exceed her personal range."

ARCHER WINSTON,
New York Post

"Barbra Streisand does something quite remarkable in *The Way We Were*, at Loew's State 1 and Tower East. She acts. I don't mean that statement to be as insulting as it sounds. It is just that in the past Miss Streisand has tended to dominate her movie roles by the sheer force of her personality. A born superstar, she has had only to be herself, to be the kind of thick-skinned but nice Jewish girl who grows in Brooklyn. Her movies have begun to seem monotonous, mostly I think because of that brittle shell she always maintains. But in *The Way We Were* that brittleness has happily disappeared. She is softer, more womanly and therefore more appealing. . . . She brings a touching vulnerability to the character of Katie, and unexpected depth. For once she is not overwhelmingly Streisand, but a thinking, feeling woman who suffers from the pain of love in a very real way."

KATHLEEN CARROLL,
New York Daily News

CUE MAGAZINE'S "ENTERTAINER OF THE YEAR"
AWARD–1963. Barbra is congratulated by Van Heflin and Eli
Wallach after receiving her citation on December 27, 1963.

GRAMMY AWARD–1964. After accepting her sec
Grammy for "People," Barbra poses with Louis Armstr
who won for his rendition of "Hello, Dolly!"

MISS ZIEGFELD OF 1965. Barbra proudly wears the cr
given her by the Ziegfeld Club, comprised of former Z
feld girls.

CUE MAGAZINE'S "ENTERTAINER OF THE YEAR"
AWARD–1969. Barbra displays both her Cue Awards at a reception in January, 1970. Directly behind her is Burt Bacharach.

EMMY AWARD. La Streisand appears to relish her Award from
the National Academy of Television Arts and Sciences after she
was cited for "Outstanding Individual Achievement in Entertainment" for My Name Is Barbra.

*MMY AWARD–1963. With (left to right) Quincy
, Jack Jones, Steve Lawrence, Eydie Gorme, Tony
ett and Count Basie after winning her first Grammy for
py Days Are Here Again."*

Gregory Peck after being named "Best Musical or Comedy Actress" of 1968 for Funny Girl.

With Clint Eastwood after both were named "World Film Favorites" of 1969.

GOLDEN GLOBE AWARDS

BARBRA'S AWARDS

Barbra Streisand is the only performer in show business history to win Broadway's Tony, recording Grammys, a television Emmy, an International Golden Globe and Hollywood's Oscar. She has won the top award in every entertainment medium in which she has performed. Although she did not win a Tony Award for either *I Can Get It For You Wholesale* or her starring role in *Funny Girl* two years later, she was voted a special Tony in 1969 as "Star of the Decade." Her Miss Marmelstein did win her the New York Drama Critics' designation as "Best Supporting Actress in a Musical," her first award of any kind.

Barbra's first solo recording, *The Barbra Streisand Album*, won her a Grammy as "Best Female Vocalist" of 1963, and she won that award in the next two years as well. Her television special *My Name Is Barbra* won her an Emmy for "Outstanding Individual Achievement in Entertainment." She was named the "Best Actress" of 1968 by the Academy of Motion Picture Arts and Sciences for *Funny Girl*.

In addition to these major accolades, Barbra has received many other coveted awards. We herewith present a selection of photographs of Barbra accepting some of the most notable of these citations.

TONY AWARD. At a reception following her presentation of a special Antoinette Perry Award as "Star of the Decade" in 1969.

ACADEMY AWARD. Barbra proudly holds her Oscar after being named "Best Actress of 1968" for Funny Girl.

FRIAR'S CLUB "ENTERTAINER OF THE YEAR" AWARD—1969. At the reception in her honor. Danny Thomas is to her right as she addresses the Friar's Club.

SAMUEL GOLDWYN AWARD. San Francisco Mayor Joseph Alioto presents Streisand with her designation as "Best Actress of 1968" for Funny Girl.

GOLDEN APPLE AWARD. With Fred Astaire after they and Diahann Carroll were named "Most Cooperative with the Press" by the Hollywood Women's Press Association in 1969

219

With Michael Sarrazin in a scene from For Pete's Sake

. . . AND INTO THE SECOND DECAD

Barbra Streisand's second decade in show business has begun in a characteristically successful way and amid a swirl of projects.

The Way We Were earned nearly 34 million dollars in its first three months of release, and will most likely go on to become Barbra's biggest hit. Streisand's recording of the title song shot up to Number One on *Billboard* magazine's "Top 100 Singles" list. A Streisand album called *The Way We Were* and the soundtrack from the film both becam best sellers.

In June 1974, Barbra's eighth movie, *For Pete's Sake*, was released. Co-starring Michael Sarrazin and Estelle Parsons, it is the story of a Broo lyn cabdriver's wife and her adventures with the stock market. Released Columbia, the film was directed by Peter Yates.

Barbra began filming a sequel to *Funny Girl* during the spring of 1974. Entitled *Funny Lady*, it will be produced by Ray Stark, directed by Herbert Ross, and released by Columbia. Dealing with Fanny Brice' later years, particularly her marriage to Billy Rose, it will co-star James Caan as Rose.

Other projects in Streisand's future include *Freaky Friday*, a musical Marty Erlichman will produce, and *With or Without Roller Skates*, a Paramount Picture about a nurse and her unorthodox methods of dealing with her patients.

A possibility for Barbra is Ingmar Bergman's *The Merry Widow*. Early in 1973, Bergman publicly announced his desire to star Streisand in the film, and she flew to Stockholm to discuss it with him. So far it is not set, but if the project does come off, considering the intensely personal styles of these two artists, the result should be fascinating.

BARBRA FILMING
FOR PETE'S SAKE

With Jason, his nurse and Director Peter Yates on location.

Michael Sarrazin during location filming in New York.

With her stand-in, Trudie Green.

Among other films being discussed for Barbra are an American International Pictures version of *Camille* and the Sarah Bernhardt film biography still being planned by Ken Russell.

Early in 1974, Barbra Streisand was named as one of the Top Ten Box Office Stars of 1973. She was the only female to make the list. Undoubtedly Hollywood's premiere actress, Barbra now has her pick of the best scripts, directors and cameramen. While no one can say for sure just where her career will take her in the next ten years, one thing is certain: she will continue to choose vehicles which help her to grow as an artist. And if her future entertainment activities are nearly as successful as her past endeavors have been, we have a great deal to look forward to.

Barbra enacts an escape down a manhole, complete with blonde wig as disguise.

With Michael Sarrazin.

Streisand